Letting Your Property

Cavendish
Publishing
Limited

London • Sydney • Portland, Oregon

This book is supported by a Companion Website, created to keep titles in the *Pocket Lawyer* series up to date and to provide enhanced resources for readers.

Key features include:

◆ forms and letters, in a ready-to-use Word format
Access all the material you need at the click of a button

◆ updates on key developments
Your book won't become out of date

◆ links to useful websites
No more fruitless internet searches

www.cavendishpublishing.com/pocketlawyer

Letting Your Property

Rosy Border & Mark Fairweather

Cavendish
Publishing
Limited

London • Sydney • Portland, Oregon

Second edition first published in Great Britain 2004 by
Cavendish Publishing Limited, The Glass House,
Wharton Street, London WC1X 9PX, United Kingdom
Telephone: + 44 (0)20 7278 8000   Facsimile: + 44 (0)20 7278 8080
Email: info@cavendishpublishing.com
Website: www.cavendishpublishing.com

Published in the United States by Cavendish Publishing
c/o International Specialized Book Services,
5824 NE Hassalo Street, Portland,
Oregon 97213-3644, USA

Published in Australia by Cavendish Publishing (Australia) Pty Ltd
45 Beach Street, Coogee, NSW 2034, Australia
Email: info@cavendishpublishing.com.au
Website: www.cavendishpublishing.com.au

The first edition of this title was originally published by The Stationery Office

British Library Cataloguing in Publication Data
Border, Rosy
Letting your property - 2nd ed - (Pocket lawyer)
1 Landlord and tenant - Great Britain
I Title II Fairweather, Mark
346.4'104346

Library of Congress Cataloguing in Publication Data
Data available

ISBN 1-85941-855-4

1 3 5 7 9 10 8 6 4 2

Printed and bound in Great Britain

Contents

PART 3
THE NITTY GRITTY

PART 4
DOCUMENTS AND INFORMATION

Disclaimer

This book puts *you* in control. This is an excellent thing, but it also makes *you* responsible for using it properly. Few washing machine manufacturers will honour their guarantee if you don't follow their 'instructions for use'. In the same way, we are unable to accept liability for any loss arising from mistakes or misunderstandings on your part. So take time to read this book carefully.

Although this book points you in the right direction, reading one small book will not make you an expert, and there are times when you may need to take advice from professionals. This book is not a definitive statement of the law, although we believe it to be accurate as at January 2004.

The authors and publisher cannot accept liability for any advice or material that becomes obsolete due to subsequent changes in the law after publication, although every effort will be made to show any changes in the law that take place after the publication date on the companion website.

About the authors

Mark Fairweather is a practising solicitor, and is one of the founding partners of the legal firm Fairweather Stephenson & Co. He and Rosy Border have written 14 books together, including five titles in Cavendish Publishing's *Pocket Lawyer* series. He has two children and lives in Suffolk.

Rosy Border, co-author of this title and series editor of the *Pocket Lawyer* series, has a first class honours degree in French and has worked in publishing, lecturing, journalism and the law. A prolific author and adapter, she stopped counting after 150 titles. She owns and manages several properties, which she describes as her 'pension fund'. Rosy and her husband, John Rabson, live in rural Suffolk and have a grown up family. Rosy enjoys DIY, entertaining and retail therapy in French markets.

Acknowledgments

A glance at the 'Useful contacts' will show the many sources we dipped into while writing this book. Thank you, everybody. We would especially like to thank Deborah Gold and the team at Shelter for their help and advice with Chapter 10, and John Rabson for IT support and refreshments.

Welcome

Welcome to *Pocket Lawyer*. Let's face it, the law is a maze and you are likely to get lost unless you have a map. This book is your map through the part of the maze that deals with letting residential property.

Important note: is this the right book for you?

This book is about landlords and *tenants*. *Taking in a Lodger* in the *Pocket Lawyer* series is about landlords and *lodgers*.

The law treats landlords with tenants differently from landlords with lodgers. Which kind of landlord are you? Turn to p 11 to find out.

We put *you* in control

This book empowers you. This is a good thing; but being in control means responsibility as well as power, so please use this book properly. Read it with care and don't be afraid to make notes – we have left wide margins for you to do just that. Take your time – do not skip anything:

o   everything is there for a purpose;
o   if anything were unimportant, we would have left it out.

Think of yourself as a driver using a road map. The map tells you the route, but it is up to you to drive carefully along it.

Sometimes you are in danger of getting out of your depth and you will need to take professional advice. Watch out for the hazard sign.

Sometimes we pause to explain something: the origin of a word, perhaps, or why a particular piece of legislation was passed. You do not need to know these things to make use of this book, but we hope you find them interesting.

Sometimes we stop to empower you to do something. Look out for the 'Power points'.

Clear English rules OK

Client to solicitor who has just drafted a contract for him: 'This *can't* be legal – I can understand it!'

Our style is WYSIWYG – what you see is what you get.

Some legal documents have traditionally been written in archaic language, often known as 'law-speak'. This term also extends to the practice of using the names of legal cases as shorthand for legal concepts. This wording has stood the test of time – often several centuries – and has been hallowed by the courts. Some of the words used sound just like everyday language, but beware – it is a kind of specialist shorthand.

Why write your tenancy agreement in a foreign language in preference to plain English? What is important is that it is legally sound and is expressed in clear, unambiguous language that accurately reflects your intentions.

When we *do* need to use technical language, we offer clear explanations: see 'Buzzwords'. These words appear in the text in **bold** so you can check their meaning.

A note on gender

This book is unisex. We acknowledge that there are both male and female members of every group and we try to allow for that in the text by using, wherever possible, the generic *they/them* rather than *he/she, him/her*, etc.

A note on Scotland and Northern Ireland

This book deals mainly with the situation in England and Wales. While the *general advice* in this book should be helpful to readers everywhere in the UK, the *legal procedure* (court procedure, forms, etc) is different in Scotland and Northern Ireland.

Click onto the website

www.cavendishpublishing.com/pocketlawyer

What this book can do for you

It can help you to rent out your house or flat. If you follow our advice you should end up with a tenancy agreement that:

o does what you want it to do;

o is legally sound;

o you as a non-lawyer can understand.

This book gives you, as landlord, the fullest protection the law can offer, combined with a fair deal for your tenant. We show how to minimise the risks for you by:

o advising you about choosing your tenant;

o advising you about vetting your tenant;

o making your tenant legally responsible for paying the rent and looking after your property;

o making sure you can get your tenant out when you want to;

o offering general advice on tax, mortgage and insurance considerations.

Additionally, this book:

o provides the general information that professional advisers would give you on the subject if only they had the time, and if only you had the money to pay them;

o   tells you the buzzwords that are important in this
    section of the law and what they mean;

o   provides samples of the letters, etc that you need;

o   answers some of the most frequently asked
    questions on the subject;

o   is supported by a regularly updated website.

What this book can't do for you

It can't guarantee that everything will go right every
time.

There will always be bad tenants, tenants who are slow
payers, tenants who damage their landlord's property or
fall out with the neighbours. A bad tenant could cost you
a lot of money as well as causing you a great deal of
stress.

Buzzwords

Here are some terms you will come across in this book. Please do not skip this section, as many of the terms used by lawyers have special meanings. Here we make them clear. The terms appear in **bold** in the text.

assured shorthold tenancy (AST) – a popular way of renting property in the private sector. Let's take it step by step. *Tenancy* means living in someone's property in exchange for rent. *Assured* in this context means that the tenancy is subject to the *statutory* framework of housing legislation. *Shorthold* means short term – well, short by some standards: the minimum period is, in effect, six months.

Buy-to-Let mortgages – loans to enable people to borrow money to buy property to rent out. The idea – in theory at least – is that the rent from the property covers the monthly payments on the loan and the potential rental income is taken into account when the lender assesses the borrower's ability to service the loan (see p 35 for a fuller explanation).

company let – a situation where a tenancy is taken on by company rather than an individual (see p 49 for the pros and cons of this arrangement).

deposit – a sum of money which the tenant hands to the landlord at the start of a tenancy to cover any unpaid rent, to pay the cost of cleaning the property when the tenant leaves and to make good any damage the tenant has done. The landlord holds the deposit and returns it (less any such deductions) to the tenant at the end of the letting period.

discretionary – a matter of free choice (unfortunately, not usually *your* choice); the opposite of *mandatory*, below.

exclusive possession – a tenant's right to occupy (that is, live in) the property they rent and to be able to lock the rest of the world out, apart from (arranged) visits for inspection, maintenance, etc. It is exclusive possession that distinguishes a *tenancy* (see below), where the tenant does have exclusive possession, from a *licence* (see below), where a *resident* landlord can come and go at will in the premises the licensee occupies.

freehold – property ownership in which you own the property for ever – unless you sell it, of course. There is no time limit, as there is with a *lease*. One other feature is that freeholders hardly ever pay rent.

ground rent – a nominal rent paid by flat owners to the owner of the building (often called the 'head landlord' or 'ground rent landlord') of which the flat forms a part. Flat owners will often pay a service charge as well, which is usually far from nominal!

habitable – fit to be lived in.

house in multiple occupation (HMO) – the Housing Act 1985 defines an HMO as 'a house which is occupied by persons who do not form a single household'. A typical example might be a large house split into several separate flats or bedsits. There are special rules about the safety and fitness of HMOs (see p 24 for details).

initial fixed period – the fixed time for which a property is let on an *AST*, after which, if both landlord and tenant agree, the property can be let for another fixed period or on a week-to-week or month-to-month basis.

Inventory – a room by room list of the contents of a property and their condition at the time of letting. The landlord and tenant go through the inventory together at the beginning of the tenancy to check that everything is there. Both sign it, and at the end of the tenancy they go through the inventory again.

jointly and severally (as in 'jointly and severally responsible/liable') – together *and* individually. Think of *severing* into several separate bits.

If two or more tenants sign a tenancy agreement, they are *jointly and severally* responsible for the rent and *jointly and severally* liable for any damage. This means that you can claim the full amount from any or from all of them.

Landlord – someone to whom a tenant pays rent in return for a tenancy in accommodation owned by the landlord.

'Land' comes from the old English for a strip of field and looms large in the legal consciousness. In the legal context, it has evolved to include bricks and mortar. The Land Registry is the modern Domesday Book, listing as it does almost all the real estate in the (sorry!) land.

lease – a legal interest in land. In this context, a contract between landlord and tenant giving the tenant *exclusive possession* (see above), for a definable limited period, of property owned by the landlord, almost invariably in exchange for rent. A lease is essentially the same as a *tenancy* (see below).

leasehold – the form of property ownership which is limited in time (for example, six months, 999 years) and is characterised by payment of rent to a landlord. Flats are usually leasehold. All tenancy agreements are forms of leasehold.

If you own a leasehold flat, you will have to pay *ground rent* to your ground rent landlord. At the end of the lease, in 99 or 999 years or whatever, the flat will revert to your landlord. For that reason, a lease is often referred to as a 'wasting asset'.

licence – a personal right to occupy property, but without rights of *exclusive possession* (see above). The commonest kind of licence is the arrangement between a resident landlord and a lodger or *licensee*, who typically has their own room and shares some facilities with the landlord.

mandatory – compulsory, the opposite of *discretionary* (see above).

notice – a formal announcement that you are going to do something, such as leave a property or repossess it.

reference – a statement about the character (and sometimes the creditworthiness) of a prospective tenant.

resident landlord – a landlord who lives in the same premises as their tenant/lodger. Resident landlords cannot in general grant *ASTs* (see above). If you are a resident landlord, you need to read *Taking in a Lodger* in the *Pocket Lawyer* series.

self-contained – a complete unit, not sharing any facilities.

statutory – laid down by law (statute) passed by Parliament, as opposed to 'judge-made' law (case law).

sub-letting – the letting by a flat owner or other tenant of all or part of property that they rent.

ten per cent wear and tear – the standard figure allowed by the Revenue in respect of annual upkeep of rental property. If your annual receipts from rent come to £3,000, you are allowed £300 a year towards maintenance even if (chance would be a fine thing!) you do not in fact spend that amount, and you do not have to say in detail how you spent the money (see p 95 for a fuller explanation).

tenancy – a typical law-speak definition is 'an arrangement under which *exclusive possession* of a property is granted for a fixed or ascertainable period of time' – almost invariably in return for rent.

There are two key elements here: the 'exclusive possession' (see above) and the 'ascertainable period of time'. The tenancy agreement has to say

o   *when* the tenancy is to start *and*

o   *when* (or how, for example 'two months' notice') it is to end.

During that 'ascertainable period of time' the tenant enjoys exclusive use of the property, as opposed to a lodger who does not. Tenants have more legal protection than lodgers.

Tenant and *tenancy* come from the Latin and old French words for 'hold'. You can hold something without owning it, so the word 'tenant' actually sums the situation up quite neatly.

Frequently asked questions (FAQs)

I want to let my house for a year while I am working abroad. How can I be sure of getting my tenant out when I come home?

Grant them an **assured shorthold tenancy (AST)**. We show you how in Chapter 2.

And what are the tax implications?

You should read the Inland Revenue's booklet IR140, *Non-resident Landlords, Their Agents and Tenants*, for guidance on income tax, available from your local tax office or from their website (see 'Useful contacts').

I want to let my house for a month while I am working abroad. How can I be sure of getting my tenant out when I come home?

One month – no can do. See below.

I want to let my house for two months while I am working abroad. How can I be sure of getting my tenant out when I come home?

The short answer is, think carefully. Is it worth it?

The long answer is that you cannot use an **AST** because it does not give you the right to take back the property from your tenant until a minimum of six months has passed. You can still let your house for two months, but first, the tenancy must not be shorthold, and secondly, you must serve written **notice** on the tenant *before the tenancy starts* that you have occupied the property as your only or principal home. The notice should make reference to Ground 1 Part 1 Schedule 2 of the Housing Act 1988. If the tenant then refuses to move out, you have to serve another notice on them – a Section 8 notice – asking for possession. The wording of the Section 8 notice is prescribed by law (creativity is not encouraged) and, in any case, must allow the tenant a further two months to leave. So, if you serve your Ground 1 and Section 8 notices at the same time, you can in theory limit the tenancy to two months. If the tenant digs their heels in, you can apply to the court for possession. There is a quickie procedure (see p 90) using form N5A, but realistically you will need to allow another two months – and if the tenant still won't go, you will need to instruct the court bailiffs to remove your tenant – another two months. Is it, cosmically speaking, worth your while?

I have a mortgage on my property. Am I allowed to let it?

Almost certainly, but you must get your mortgage lender's agreement first. Some mortgage lenders extort an annual fee for the paperwork that they say this involves. Up to £100 is usual, and they add it to your mortgage, so you don't have any choice in the matter. The lender may also increase the interest rate – in which case, consider moving to a different mortgage lender. Take care, however, to ensure that the new loan attracts tax relief. Moving lender is not a DIY matter. Seek professional advice to avoid making a saving in one area and wasting money in another.

Does a tenancy have to be for a fixed period, or can it run indefinitely?

Both are possible. You can have a *fixed term* **tenancy**, which lasts for a fixed number of weeks, months or years, or a *periodic* **tenancy**, which runs indefinitely from one rent period to the next. In practice, once the initial fixed period of an AST has passed, the letting can continue as a periodic tenancy for as long as it suits both landlord and tenant.

I own a flat in a 99 year lease. Can I rent it out?

Yes, provided your **lease** allows you to do so. If in doubt, check with your **ground rent** landlord (see p xiv). You should also check with your buildings insurers, and separately with your contents insurers if they are different, to make sure that your policies cover letting (see 'Are you insured?', p 32).

Do I need to instruct a solicitor to draw up an assured shorthold tenancy agreement?

No. If you follow our instructions carefully you will end up with a legally sound **AST**.

My house is owned by a housing association. I shall be working in Wales for a year and would like to sub-let my home. Is this allowed?

Probably; it depends on the terms of your **lease**. You will almost certainly need to ask your housing association's permission, and you should also check with the buildings and contents insurers that the property will be covered during the letting (see 'Are you insured?', p 32).

I have been told that if I let an unfurnished property it is harder to get tenants out than if I let it furnished. Is this so?

Not any more. For many years there has been no distinction between furnished and unfurnished property from the point of view of ease of eviction. Today it is the kind of tenancy you grant, not the furniture, that governs this. Our **AST** Agreement applies to both furnished and unfurnished property.

Can I charge a deposit, and what would be a reasonable amount?

Yes, you can – a month's rent would be quite normal. Read all about deposits in Chapter 12.

Do I need to provide a rent book?

Only if the rent is payable on a weekly basis. You must, however, keep a record of all rent payments. It is also a good idea to provide receipts to avoid disagreements later (see p 83 for advice).

Who is responsible for repairing 'baths, bogs, boilers and basins' – me or my tenant?

You are. You are responsible for the fabric of the building, heating and hot water installations (unless, of course, it was your tenant who did the damage) (see p 24 for details).

I have inherited my late father's house and I would like to rent it out, but I am worried about paying a lot of tax. Can you advise?

Without knowing your precise details, no. The general rule is that you will pay tax if, after deducting your expenses, your net letting income comes to more than your personal tax allowances. There is general advice on tax from p 93 below. The smart thing to do, however, is to visit the Inland Revenue website (see 'Useful contacts') and pick up all the free literature available. Alternatively, seek professional advice. A good accountant could save you serious money; consider instructing one for your first let, then going it alone if you feel confident enough.

Do I need to instruct a letting agent?

No. Many landlords do it themselves, although it is sensible to instruct an agent if, for example, you will be out of the country or frantically busy. We tell you the pros and cons of DIY or agent in Chapter 7.

If I sell a rental property and make a profit, shall I have to pay Capital Gains Tax?

Yes, unless the capital profit is small, or reliefs and exemptions apply. The annual exemption for individuals is £8,200 (tax year 2004/05). The other main relief is 'taper relief' – the concept being that the longer you own the asset, the lower the rate of tax (see p 97 for more information).

What records will I have to keep?

For the Inland Revenue, you must keep details of rents receivable/received and money paid out in respect of the rental property. You have to keep this information for six years after the tax year in question (see 'Collecting the rent and keeping track', p 83).

What rights of access to my rental property do I have as a landlord?

You, or anyone acting for you (for example, a workman), have only whatever rights your Tenancy Agreement gives you. Usually a tenancy agreement will give you the right to enter the property at reasonable times of day to do any repairs that are your responsibility, and also to inspect the property. You will usually be required to give 24 hours' **notice** of any inspection. All this is set out in the Tenancy Agreement in Chapter 17. Note that entering the property without the right to do so, or without giving notice, may amount to harassment.

I read somewhere that I had to have a deed in order to rent out my property. Is this right?

No – unless the agreement is for a fixed period of three years or more.

I have a flat in Knightsbridge which I am thinking of letting out at £500 per week. Can I use an AST?

£500 a week – hmm, that comes to £26,000 a year. Sorry, it won't be an **AST**, because the **statutory regime** applies only to lettings where the annual rent is £25,000 or less. This is more a problem for your tenant than for you, as you will be able to apply for possession within the first six months – if that is what you and the tenant agree. (In other words, because this is not an AST, your tenant does not enjoy the AST's initial period (eg six months) during which you, the landlord, cannot repossess.)

I have tenants in a mobile home park. What rights do they have?

It depends whether you are letting the pitch on which the mobile home stands, or the mobile home itself.

If you are letting the pitch, the tenant has extensive **statutory** protection under the Mobile Homes Act 1983 – which is a law unto itself!

If you are letting the mobile home on the pitch, the letting is subject to the same law as applies to other residential lettings. In other words, you can give your tenants an **AST**. Do bear in mind your fitness, safety and repair obligations (see Chapter 3). Mobile homes *must* be fitted with smoke alarms.

According to the Office of the Deputy Prime Minister, we don't talk about 'mobile homes' any more. We have to call them 'park homes'!

I own a cottage in the Dordogne and am considering letting it for six months or more. Can I use an AST?

No, because **AST**s are governed by the law of England and Wales. Your cottage is in France and would come under French law.

PART I

BEFORE YOU LET YOUR PROPERTY

You are making history

From the earliest times until the end of World War I almost everybody, even the very rich, rented their homes. Remember Jane Austen's *Pride and Prejudice*:

> 'My dear Mr Bennet,' said his lady to him one day, 'have you heard that Netherfield Park is let at last? … a young man of large fortune from the north of England.'

In the days when most homes were rented from private landlords (local authority housing is a recent development – see below), the landlord could be your guardian angel – like the great philanthropists Titus Salt and Robert Owen – or a bogeyman (when you are tired of 19th century novelists, dip into Catherine Cookson's *The Dwelling Place*) to his tenants. When the landlord was also the farmer, mine owner or factory owner and the house went with the job, the death or dismissal of the breadwinner could make the whole family homeless.

After the First World War, 'social housing' became common. Local authorities built low-rent housing for people who could not afford to buy their own homes. The tenants of a local authority had much more security than tenants of a private landlord. For example, it was a lot harder for a local authority, with their obligation to follow due legal process, to evict someone than for a rascally landlord, who could just send the boys round to change the locks (see 'A new word', below).

Council houses routinely offered modern conveniences – flush lavatories, running water, electricity and so on – that privately rented homes did not. People moved gratefully into three-bedroom semis with little gardens back and front, or bright, cheerful council flats with their own bathrooms. The council, unlike a great many private landlords, on the whole took care of all the repairs (although everyone knows of estates where this didn't happen).

Private landlords' failure to maintain their property satisfactorily was not always a matter of callous indifference. In many cases the money was simply not available. Councils could put up the rates to finance repairs, so the whole private and business population subsidised the council tenants. Private landlords did not have this option. You can't get blood out of a stone and the rental income of a property regularly fell short of the cost of maintaining and repairing it. Even good landlords, therefore, could find themselves unable to supply their tenants with decent accommodation.

While local authorities were doing their bit for the housing shortage, a number of individuals and groups were also getting in on the act. Prince Albert had started a trend in the 19th century with his 'Model Artisan's Dwelling House' and a number of wealthy philanthropists followed suit in providing decent, affordable accommodation for the 'deserving poor'. Fine – they had income from other sources.

A new word

Thus public and private landlords co-existed, not always harmoniously. Then, in the 1950s, a Polish immigrant called Peter Rachman took advantage of the wave of West Indians who were invited to come to Britain to work. Rachman bought up hundreds of slum properties in Notting Hill and Bayswater for derisory sums and let them to West Indians. Prejudice and discrimination (there was no racial equality legislation in those days) meant that the new arrivals could not get any other place to live. Rachman welcomed them all. He also bullied, molested, overcharged and overcrowded his tenants and subjected them to a reign of terror. There were no laws to protect them from Rachman and his bully boys and they had nowhere else to go.

Rachman died from a heart attack in his early forties, but not before his name had entered the English language, alongside Mr Guillotin's beheading device and Mr Biro's pen. New laws were passed to protect tenants from mistreatment, but not before *Rachmanism* – defined in the OED as 'exploitation of slum tenants by unscrupulous landlords' – had entered our language.

So, fuelled in part by the Rachman scandal, legislation was enacted.

The decline of the private landlord

Landlords no longer had the right to turn out their tenants into the howling gale in a fit of pique. Tenants were given the right, if they felt that their rent was too high or that the landlord was not maintaining the property adequately, to apply for a 'fair rent' or an order for the landlord to carry out repairs.

The trouble with a 'fair rent' was that it was usually a lot lower than the going rate, and that meant even less money available for repairs than ever before. At the same time, many tenants became *regulated* or *controlled* tenants. The practical effect of this was that their landlords could neither evict them nor raise their rents. As late as the 1980s there were people who were paying only a few pounds a week to rent property which, if only their landlord could sell it with vacant possession, would fetch hundreds of thousands of pounds. Empty, the property was worth a fortune; tenanted, it was unsaleable.

What we are looking at here is a shift in the balance of power. Where once the system favoured the private landlord, often to a quite grotesque extent, by the 1960s landlords were desperate to get rid of their tenanted accommodation for whatever it would fetch, simply to shed the burden of property which brought them no income and which they could not afford to maintain.

Gradually the pool of property available for ordinary private rental dried up, until the only properties offered were the pits: damp, unmodernised and deeply unattractive.

You can't really blame the landlords. Would you want to be responsible for property which you could not afford to repair, with no chance of evicting bad tenants or getting a reasonable rent?

At the same time, with cheap mortgages which attracted tax relief more and more ordinary people were buying their own homes. By 1990 only 7% of housing in Britain was privately rented; the other 93% was either local authority/housing association property or privately owned (usually with a mortgage).

A few landlords found a way round the problem by granting 'holiday lets' for a month at a time, although in practice they could be renewed almost indefinitely. This was against the law, but there was such a dire shortage of rental accommodation that the law did not want to know.

The rise of the letting agent

There were two other kinds of landlord, however. First of all, there was Mr Mobile. Typically, Mr Mobile had landed a well paid short term contract a long way from home and needed to let his home in Britain for a year or so to finance accommodation near his new place of work. Homes like this tended to be very desirable. Their owners were naturally choosy about whom they let them to, and anxious to be able to move into their homes again when their work contract came to an end.

The second kind of landlord was less fortunate. Mr and Mrs Relocation also needed to move house to be near Mr Relocation's new job, but they were moving permanently, not on a short term basis like Mr Mobile. They had bought their home at a time when house prices were high. Falling house prices (remember the recession in the late 1980s?) meant that the Relocations owed more to their mortgage lender than their house was currently worth. So they were unable to do what they wanted to do, which was sell their existing home to finance the purchase of a similar property in the new location. The term for this situation was 'negative equity', and it was a nightmare, because if you did sell your home you would still owe the mortgage lender many thousands of pounds.

There was only one way out, and that was to let this unsaleable property until house prices rose again, and meanwhile possibly rent somewhere in their new location.

In response to these needs, a new life form evolved: the *letting agent*. Soon a new 'professional body', the **Association of Residential Letting Agents** (see 'Useful contacts'), was set up to advise them. The landlords supplied the property and the agents accepted the responsibility of managing it, often charging both landlord and tenant for doing so.

The assured shorthold tenancy (AST)

The Housing Act 1988 became law in January 1989 and turned the whole private rental sector upside down. The Act aimed to give both landlords and tenants a fairer deal and to make more properties available for rent. It introduced a new and attractive concept: a legally binding agreement which allowed properties to be rented for short bursts, typically six months at a time. There were five 'good things' about the new tenancy from the landlord's point of view:

o   the landlord could charge a market rent;

o   the Agreement committed the tenant to pay the rent for the whole of the six months even if they did not stay the full time;

o   after the initial six months, the tenant could stay on for another fixed term or for an indefinite period, which could be terminated by two months' notice from the landlord and whatever notice period the Agreement required from the tenant;

o   the landlord was sure of getting the tenant out. Even if a tenant refused to budge and a court order was needed to get them out, the court would have to grant the order provided the paperwork was correct;

o   rent increases could be imposed after the first year, though no more than one increase in any 12 month period.

Landlords realised that they would no longer be stuck with either artificially low rents or unevictable tenants and responded favourably. Safety regulations were now in force, which may have made Rachman turn in his grave but which have probably saved many lives. You can read about these regulations in Chapter 3.

The law relating to **AST**s was amended by the Housing Act 1996. The main effects of the 1996 Act are as follows:

o   an AST is the default form of residential tenancy. Unless the tenancy is a continuation of a previous letting which was not an AST, or you agree with your tenant that the letting will not be an AST, or it is a form of letting which cannot be an AST (for example, a holiday let or lodger agreement), it will be an AST by default;

o   there is no longer a minimum six month period of letting, but unless the tenant has broken the terms of the tenancy the landlord cannot repossess the property for six months anyway;

o   although an AST agreement can be made orally (unwise!), the tenant is entitled to a written statement of the principal terms.

Letting for profit

A new breed of landlord has evolved in recent years, thanks in some part to the belief (misguided or otherwise!) that property increases in value in the long term, and thanks also to the **Buy-to-Let** scheme. This scheme was dreamed up by the Association of Residential Letting Agents and a group of sympathetic mortgage lenders.

Previously it was difficult to borrow money to buy property to rent out because mortgage lenders favoured owner-occupiers, and other lenders (such as banks) charged high interest. It seemed to be considered immoral to borrow money to buy rental property. Even renting out your own home, if it was mortgaged, required the lender's special permission. Buy-to–Let is different. It is intended specifically to enable people to buy property to let. In fact, you are not supposed to live in a Buy-to-Let financed property yourself (more about Buy-to-Let in Chapter 6).

Modern landlords – and modern tenants

There are rascally landlords still lurking in the darker corners of the private rented sector, but most private landlords nowadays are decent people who would not turn a family out in the snow even if the law allowed them to.

Some own several properties, all bought for cash in a down-at-heel state, which they have renovated and equipped to a high standard: 'I never had a doll's house as a child; this is the grown-up version.'

Some see bricks and mortar as a surer long term investment than stocks and shares: 'My properties are my pension fund.'

Whatever their motives, landlords like these are doing a good job – and adding to the pool of property for rent.

At the same time, different people are choosing to rent.

For a time there seemed to be a stigma attached to renting. When council tenants were given the right to buy their homes, often at very low prices, the percentage of owner-occupiers rocketed. Anyone who was anybody, or aspired to be anybody, scraped a deposit together to 'own' their home, even if in reality all they owned was a huge millstone of debt and the doubtful privilege of repairing their own roof and rodding their own drains. But times change. As W S Gilbert says,

> When everyone is Somebody,
> Then no one's Anybody ...

and so renting became socially acceptable again.

We are not sure whether official statistics will bear this out, but we have the impression that with the rise in marriage break-ups there are a great many people from all walks of life looking for property to rent. If your marriage has gone sour and your ex is living in the former family home with the children, you may not have the wherewithal to get on the housing ladder again, and you may not want the responsibility of home ownership because you are not sure of your long term plans, so you rent.

Then there are the professionals. Young single people rent something smart and clean and labour-saving because, although they could afford to buy, they do not want the chores or the long term commitment, and they do not see why they should put down a five-figure sum as a deposit on something which may turn out to be in the wrong place. They'd rather have a car!

Or a family man lands his dream job, a long way from home. He doesn't want to uproot his family, who are doing just fine where they are, so he rents somewhere near his work and goes home to his family at weekends. His only outlay is the deposit on his rented property, and that is returnable.

ASTs suit all these 'new tenants' perfectly. Are *you* ready to be a 'new landlord'?

2

The assured shorthold tenancy explained

Are you a resident or a non-resident landlord?

All residential tenancies are subject to **statutory** control. This means that you do not have complete freedom to agree anything you like with your tenant. The legal framework is, however, different for *tenants* on the one hand and *lodgers* on the other. You need to establish which kind of landlord you are. Answer the questions below.

Do you live somewhere other than the property you are letting?

If the answer is 'yes', you are a *non-resident landlord* and the **assured shorthold tenancy** (**AST**) Agreement, which is explained here and provided in Chapter 17, is for you.

Is the accommodation you are planning to let self-contained, even if you live under the same roof?

If the answer is 'yes', you are still a *non-resident landlord* and the AST agreement is for you too.

Do you plan to let rooms in your home with shared facilities?

By 'shared facilities' we mean kitchens, bathrooms, utility rooms and so on – halls, stairs and landings don't count. If the answer is 'yes', you are a *resident landlord* and you are at the wrong party. An AST would not work for you. You need *Taking in a Lodger* in this series.

What does the assured shorthold tenancy mean in plain English? Well, 'tenancy' means living in someone's property in exchange for rent; 'assured' means the tenancy is subject to the **statutory** framework of housing legislation; 'Shorthold' means short term – but see below on what this really means.

Unless the tenant has broken the terms of the tenancy, the landlord cannot repossess the property within six months. In practice, most ASTs start with an **initial fixed period**. There is no upper limit, but six months to one year would be normal. There is a balance here between flexibility and security of income. If, however, you grant the tenancy for more than 12 months, there may be adverse tax implications (see p 96). Also, you need to make sure that you include the right to review the rent.

Moreover, if you grant a tenancy for more than three years, the tenancy agreement must be in the form of a 'deed'. In practice, this means that the signatures must be witnessed and the document must bear the words 'Signed by [insert landlord's name or tenant's name] as a deed in the presence of [insert witness's name, address and occupation]'.

After the fixed term – the six months, one year or whatever – you can either renew the letting for another fixed period or allow the letting to continue indefinitely on a periodic basis (usually month to month). If you are renewing for a fixed period, you will need a fresh tenancy agreement. Otherwise you do not need to take any action to continue the letting, apart from making the tenant aware that you are continuing on the same terms as the original letting except that you are no longer talking about a fixed term. To end the letting, see 'Getting them out', p 87).

The tenant is responsible for paying the rent for the whole of the initial period even if they leave early. In practice, if you find a replacement you may decide to let them off the hook, but it is not obligatory.

You can grant an AST which does not have an initial fixed period – but remember that unless the tenant breaks the terms of the tenancy, it will still be six months before you can repossess the property.

If your proposed tenant is already living in property owned by you on some basis other than an AST, it may not be possible for you to grant them an AST.

If this applies to you, please take expert advice, as it is not a DIY matter.

If the rent you are charging is higher than the going rate for comparable property in your area, your tenant can apply to a Rent Assessment Committee for the rent to be reduced in line with the going rate. It is, however, open to you to take steps to terminate the tenancy at the earliest opportunity, but in general this cannot be earlier than the date when your fixed term ends.

You cannot make your tenant leave until the end of the initial period at the very earliest, unless your tenant has failed to keep their side of the bargain. To repossess your property, you must give the tenant a **statutory notice**, the Notice of Landlord's Intention to Apply for Possession, which you will find on p 133 of this book. Unless you are seeking possession because the tenant is at fault, you will not be entitled to have your property back until at least two months after the tenant has received your notice (see pp 87–89).

If the tenant refuses to move out, you must get a court order to take back your property. Do not try removing them by force without a court order: that is a criminal offence. So is harassing your tenant. If you do evict your tenant unlawfully, you can be made to pay substantial compensation.

Harassment can take many forms. Here are just a few examples of hostile acts by landlords which have fallen foul of the Protection from Eviction Act 1977:

o   kicking the tenant's door every time you go past;
o   sabotaging their hot water supply or blocking their lavatory;
o   turning off the gas, electricity or water without good cause;
o   removing slates from the roof;
o   taking up floorboards every weekend on the pretext of repairing the electric wiring.

An AST means you can get the tenants out when their time's up without sending the boys round. Even if your tenants dig their heels in and refuse to budge, the court *must* find in your favour provided you have got your paperwork right. So you can skip the sabotage.

Is your property safe?

As landlord of a residential property, you have **statutory** duties (duties that you cannot dodge, even if your tenant is on your side) to provide your tenant with accommodation which is safe. Nor can you turn a blind eye to safety issues. You can be made criminally liable for unsafe property even if you are not aware of the hazards.

Safety regulations are the invisible underside of a massive iceberg. Most of us know that there are laws to protect us from dangerous products and practices, but we are unaware of the vast body of regulations required to do this. See what we mean about an iceberg? Dive under every heading in this chapter and you will find the statutory instruments that spell out the law on that subject in all its labyrinthine complexity. It is not realistic for you, the landlord, to be familiar with every statutory instrument that might apply, but you must be alert to health and safety issues. In the end, ignorance is no excuse. Get a professional in to check for hazards that you lack the knowledge to spot for yourself.

Electrical safety

> The rule: your electrical wiring and installations must be safe, and so must all electrical appliances.

The Landlord and Tenant Act 1985 requires you to ensure that the *electrical installations* are safe when the tenancy begins and that they are kept that way throughout the tenancy. Electrical appliances (as opposed to fixed installations) come under the Electrical Equipment (Safety) Regulations 1994. It is an offence not only to sell dodgy electrical appliances (which is why you seldom see old toasters in charity shops nowadays) but also to let property containing such items. Make sure your plugs and sockets comply with modern standards – old round-pin plugs are suspect. Modern 13 amp flat pin plugs should be marked as complying with British Standard BS1363, and they must contain correctly rated fuses.

Surprisingly, although you have this legal duty to ensure that your rental property is electrically safe, there is no compulsory scheme along the lines of the gas safety scheme (see below). Do not, however, wait for legislation to catch up with common sense. You should have your property checked for electrical safety before you let it, and at regular intervals afterwards. This includes

o   wiring circuits and sockets, and
o   all electrical appliances.

The Institution of Electrical Engineers recommend the following test intervals:

o   fixed electrical installations – five years;
o   household appliances – visual check every six months, full inspection every 12 months.

There are over 2,000 electric shock accidents and over 9,000 electrical fires in homes in the UK every year. Here is a checklist of electrical safety hazards from Trading Standards, any one of which could injure or even kill someone.

o   Frayed or damaged cables.
o   Old appliances with metal parts and no earth.
o   Electric fires with fireguards whose openings are too wide (more than 25 mm x 12 mm or 50 mm x 20 mm for silicon covered elements).
o   Installations with damage allowing access to live parts (for example, damaged plugs).
o   Lamp sockets with no shielding for the metal part of the bulb.
o   Loose or worn connectors (for example, kettle sockets).
o   Evidence of overheating.
o   Wires disconnected.
o   Wrong fuses used.

o   Old type wiring (red, green and black instead of the modern brown, blue and green/yellow stripes).

o   Incorrect plugs or non-working cord grips.

This is a horrifying list. Any one of these electrical faults could start a fire.

You may already know a reliable electrician. If not, the National Inspection Council for Electrical Installation Contractors (see 'Useful contacts') approves electrical contractors who issue detailed electrical safety reports and, if any remedial work is done, provide signed certificates. At the time of writing, many university accommodation officers are already insisting on electrical safety certificates.

You may be able to arrange an electrical safety check free of charge. Contact your own electricity supplier in the first instance (there should be a display ad in your local telephone directory). They should be able to give you a freephone number to call.

Beware tenants who import dodgy electrical equipment into your property. The cautious approach is to supply your own appliances – and make sure they are listed in your inventory.

Gas safety

> **The rule: if there is gas in your property, it must be safe.**

Carbon monoxide gas from poorly installed or badly maintained gas appliances and flues kills about 30 people every year. As a landlord you are responsible for the safety of your tenants. You have a responsibility under the Gas Safety (Installation and Use) Regulations 1998 to have all gas appliances, flues and other fittings checked to make sure they are safe and working satisfactorily. These checks *must* be carried out not less than every 12 months, and checking isn't enough – you *must* have any repair work or servicing done that the installer says is needed. You have a duty to make sure that:

o   gas fittings (appliances and pipework) and flues are maintained in a safe condition;

o   all installation, maintenance and safety checks must be carried out by a CORGI-registered (Council for Registered Gas Installers) gas installer;

o   a CORGI-registered gas installer must carry out an annual safety check on every gas appliance (nobody else will do);

o   a record of each safety check is kept for two years;

o   a copy of the current safety check record must be issued to each tenant within 28 days of the check being completed, or to each new tenant before they move in;

o   gas appliances – cookers, gas fires and boilers – must comply with modern safety standards. Any appliance which is more than 10 years old needs checking (which is where your CORGI installer comes in).

The statutory maintenance and safety requirements do not apply to appliances owned by your tenant, nor to flues or chimneys solely connected to appliances owned by your tenant. All the same, it is sensible to get those checked too in case your tenant sets fire to your property or tries to blame any disasters on you.

Checks must have taken place within a year of the start of the tenancy, unless the appliances are less than one year old, in which case they must be inspected within 12 months of their installation date. When your CORGI installer has given your gas installations the all-clear, you will be given two copies of a gas safety certificate, one for you and one for your tenant. Keep your copy on file and pass the other to your tenant within 28 days.

Checking your gas installation is not a DIY job. You *must* call in a CORGI installer (see 'Useful contacts').

Ensuring gas safety is not a job you can delegate to your tenant! The responsibility is yours alone. Failure to comply with the regulations could land you in court, facing a fine of up to £5,000. If someone is killed or injured by your negligence in this respect, you could face an unlimited fine or even prison.

Always note in your diary the date when your gas safety certificate falls due for renewal. It is all too easy to let it lapse, which would mean breaking the law.

Fire safety

The rule: In general terms, your property must not present a fire risk.

---

o   Flats: flats and bedsits must have adequate means of escape in case of fire.
o   Smoke alarms: properties built since 1992 must have mains powered smoke alarms fitted from new. It is your responsibility as landlord to ensure at the start of the letting that the alarms are in working order. For older properties, we take the view that you should at least supply battery powered smoke alarms. Test them and start the letting with fresh batteries. Smoke alarms are compulsory in **HMOs** and caravans.
o   Upholstered furniture must be flame retardant.

The law (Furniture and Furnishings (Fire) (Safety) Regulations 1988 as amended 1993) requires that all furniture in any property rented to new tenants after 1 January 1997 must comply with the Regulations. Since 1988 all *new* upholstered furniture has had to pass exacting safety tests, and since 1993 the requirements were extended to apply to *secondhand* furniture. However, there is still a lot of 'illegal' furniture about, made from untreated polyurethane foam, which catches fire very easily and gives off poisonous fumes.

You can have as much flammable furniture as you like in your own home, but you will be breaking the law unless the soft furnishings in your rental accommodation are flame retardant. Turn the item upside down and look for the label. A typical label will say something along the lines of 'CARELESSNESS CAUSES FIRE' and carry a batch number. These labels are usually sewn in. If the furniture was manufactured before 1988 it is most unlikely to comply with the regulations.

Interestingly, there are gaps in this legislation. Although the regulations cover beds, headboards, mattresses, sofa beds, futons, cushions and pillows as well as upholstered furniture, they make no mention of curtains, bedding including duvets, curtains or carpets.

There is a free leaflet available, *A Guide to the Furniture and Furnishings (Fire) (Safety) Regulations* (see 'Useful contacts).

1   If you are doubtful whether any of the furniture in your rental property complies with the regulations, your local trading standards department should be able to advise.

2   Whatever type of residential property you let, you should consider asking your local fire prevention officer (FPO) (whose number will be in your local telephone directory) to check it out for fire safety. This service will normally be available free of charge. Take careful note of the FPO's findings *and act on them*. A fire blanket by the kitchen stove and a smoke alarm on the landing cost very little – some local fire departments even provide them free of charge – and could save lives.

Risk management

> The rule: apart from the specific points above, your property must be safe for your tenants and their visitors.

Try to minimise the accident potential of the property you propose to let, together with the contents of a furnished let. The buzzword is *risk management*. Go round your property checking for possible hazards such as:

o   dodgy window catches;
o   loose bits of carpet, especially on stairs;
o   trailing cables;

o splinters in wooden surfaces;

o loose floorboards;

o old furniture that might not meet modern safety standards – for example, bunk beds made before 1987 which might injure an unwary child.

Make a record of your inspection and note any action taken. If you have serious doubts about whether your property meets current standards of fitness and/or safety, your local housing authority may inspect it for you. Local authorities want property to be available for letting in their district and most are happy to do this free of charge.

Having made sure your property and the contents are safe, you must also keep them that way throughout the tenancy.

Is your property habitable?

As landlord of a residential property, you have a **statutory** duty, which the local housing authority can enforce, to provide your tenant with accommodation which is **habitable**.

This means the property must:

o   be structurally stable;

o   be free from serious disrepair;

o   be free from dampness prejudicial to the occupant's health;

o   have adequate provision for lighting, heating and ventilation;

o   have an adequate supply of clean water;

o   have satisfactory cooking and food preparation facilities, including a sink with hot and cold water;

o   have a suitably located lavatory for the tenant's exclusive use;

o   have a suitably located fixed bath or shower and wash hand basin with hot and cold water for the tenant's exclusive use;

o   have an effective drainage system.

Where flats are concerned, the one you are letting must not be an island of excellence in a sea of squalor: the whole building must comply with the main fitness requirements.

At the time of writing, there are proposals to replace these existing fitness standards (which have gradually evolved over a period of 80 years) with a new Housing Health and Safety Rating System. You can find out more about this on the website of the Office of the Deputy Prime Minister (see 'Useful contacts'). More information about the current fitness standards is at Annex F of the ODPM's leaflet, *A Decent Home*, also available online.

All this may sound daunting and possibly expensive, but you might qualify for help in the form of a local authority or central government grant (see 'A word on grants', below).

Is your property in good nick?

You have the following **statutory** duties, which the tenant can enforce (under the Landlord and Tenant Act 1985):

o   to keep the structure and exterior of the property in repair. This includes drains, gutters and external pipes;

o   to keep the water supply and sanitation in good repair. This includes basins, sinks, baths and what the Act charmingly calls 'sanitary conveniences';

o   to keep the space-heating and water-heating installations in good working order.

As above, if this sounds daunting and possibly expensive, you might qualify for help in the form of a local authority or central government grant (see 'A word on grants', below).

A note on HMOs

HMOs are 'houses in multiple occupation'. An HMO is defined in the legislation as *'a house which is occupied by persons who do not form a single household'*. An example of an HMO would be a large house converted into separate flats or bedsits, with several individuals or families living as separate households under one roof. Much student accommodation is in the form of HMOs, although the boundaries between single and multiple households are blurred, particularly where students are concerned! For example, the exact number of occupants needed for a house to be classed as an HMO varies from one local authority to another.

Purpose-built blocks of flats are generally regarded as outside HMO territory. The main thrust of the legislation is directed at older properties that have been converted into bedsits and small flats. This type of accommodation presents increased risks to the people living there, particularly fire risks – five kitchen stoves are by definition five times as risky as one, and dodgy loft conversions can be death traps.

HMOs must comply with ordinary housing fitness and safety standards (see above). In addition, the following fitness standards apply specifically to HMOs, which must have:

o   satisfactory food preparation and cooking facilities;
o   adequate toilet provision;
o   adequate washing/bathing facilities including hot and cold water;
o   adequate fire escapes;
o   adequate fire precautions, including smoke alarms.

In addition:

o   most local housing authorities have registration schemes for HMOs on their patch, so if you think you may be letting an HMO you need to ask your local housing department whether you need to register. Registration may be conditional upon carrying out improvements or agreeing to manage your HMO according to the local authority's rules (for example, relating to overcrowding);
o   managers of HMOs have a duty 'to maintain the common parts and installations', and failure to do so is a criminal offence;
o   special fire safety standards apply to HMOs of three or more storeys;
o   HMOs built or converted since 1991 must comply with the 1991 Building Regulations.

At the time of writing, the government is proposing a new national licensing scheme for HMOs. For further details, see the consultation paper issued by the Office of the Deputy Prime Minister under the title 'Licensing of Houses in Multiple Occupation – England', available online at the ODPM website (see 'Useful contacts'). It is worth checking whether your local authority has a website and, if so, what it has to say about HMOs.

Dangerous, dodgy and decaying?

If you let property which is unsafe and/or unfit and/or in disrepair, you can get into serious trouble. If the worst happens and someone dies or is injured, the victims may be able to sue you for compensation and you might be criminally liable as well.

Meanwhile, depending on the problem, the local authority, your tenant or both of them together can compel you to carry out remedial work.

Local authorities have duties and powers under the Housing Act 1985 to ensure that properties in their district are fit for human habitation and to take action to put matters right. Where tenanted property is concerned, they can serve an enforcement **notice** under the Housing Act 1985 on you or your agent. They can charge up to £300 for doing this.

If you do not get the repairs done yourself, the local authority has the power to get it done and pass on their costs to you – and in serious cases to prosecute you as well.

The council does not have to tell you how they found out about your substandard property, so anyone – your tenant, your nosy neighbour, your disgruntled ex – can rat on you. It simply isn't worth the risk – *make sure your property is habitable before you rent it out*.

In the case of furnished property, the tenant can also take action against you if the property is 'unfit for human habitation'. Specifically, the property must be free of vermin and insect infestation when the letting starts.

This archaic distinction between furnished and unfurnished property derives from the 1843 case of *Smith v Marrable*. The house was furnished. It was infested with bugs. The court ruled that the landlord was in breach of an implied obligation that the house should be reasonably fit for human habitation. We can't see why landlords of unfurnished property should not be under the same obligation. It is surely time for this to be tested in the courts!

A word on grants

You might qualify for a grant to bring your property up to standard. These grants are meant to help landlords to:

o   make their properties fit for human habitation;

o   upgrade habitable properties which need substantial repair;

o   provide fire protection and escape (for self-contained flats);

o   improve heating and thermal insulation (for example, lofts, tanks, cavity walls, double glazing);

o   improve energy efficiency;

o   improve fire safety (for all properties).

Before you become too excited, however, we should point out that grants usually have strings attached. The grant process is very involved and you will probably have to jump through a great many hoops before the authorities will part with any money. Moreover, you will not be allowed to start work until the grant has been approved, which might wreck your timetable.

There is, however, no harm in trying. You can start by calling your local council and asking to speak to someone from the private sector housing team.

Another, probably surer, source of help would be one of the energy saving schemes subsidised by central government in association with the various utilities. Many private landlords have had cavity wall insulation and loft lagging done for a fraction of the real cost. Provision seems to vary from area to area: ask around.

One bonus of having a tenant who is receiving benefits is that you would be likely to qualify for *free* home improvements under 'Warm Front', the government's Home Energy Efficiency Scheme. For example, a tenant over 60 years of age and in receipt of benefits might well qualify your property for a complete *free* central heating system with no strings attached except a promise not to raise the rent for one year after completion of the work.

Many landlords have had thousands of pounds' worth of free work done under this scheme (call 0800 952 1555 for details).

Your tenant's obligations

Your tenant has obligations to use your property in a responsible way. For instance, if they are going away in winter they should turn off the water to avoid possible burst pipes. They should unblock the sink when it gets clogged up. They should not damage your property, or let anyone else do so.

What's more, if the tenants notice that anything is amiss for which you are responsible, they need to tell you. Our Tenancy Agreement provides for them to do this.

Suppose your tenant tries to withhold rent because you are slow in carrying out repairs? If the disrepair is causing the tenant genuine inconvenience or presents a health hazard, they might have a point! Try not to get into this situation in the first place.

In theory, you could take the tenant to court for rent arrears, or even evict them after serving the proper **notice** (see p 133). The practical approach, however, is to get the work done one way or another. If your tenant is anxious to get the repairs done quickly, you can agree with them that they will get the work done and deduct the cost from the rent, passing the receipted invoices to you, but this is something you must decide between you.

What if a tenant tries a spot of DIY repair work and gets it wrong? The law says they must put things right, or pay for someone else to do so.

Don't let all this worry you. The Tenancy Agreement in this book sets out the rights and duties of both you and your tenant.

Optional items

You do *not* have a statutory duty to provide furniture, carpets or curtains even for a 'furnished' property. Believe it or not, all those things are optional items to be agreed between you and your tenant.

Five star landlords?

The Office of the Deputy Prime Minister is promoting landlord accreditation schemes, run by local councils to recognise and reward good landlords on their patch.

Becoming an accredited landlord is like earning a Blue Flag for your beach or a rosette for your restaurant. According to the ODPM, accredited landlords will benefit from:

o   being publicly identified as good landlords;

o   distancing themselves from incompetent or unscrupulous landlords;

o   being able to advertise their accredited status to attract tenants who value good quality accommodation and competent management.

You can read all about it in the ODPM's leaflet, *Landlord Accreditation*, available online (see 'Useful contacts').

From a purely self-interested point of view, in a buyer's market accreditation ought to encourage potential tenants to come to you rather than to non-accredited landlords in your area.

Is there a landlord accreditation scheme in your district? Rosy called her local council, who had heard of the scheme but had no plans to introduce one on their patch.

That's rural Suffolk for you! Salford's accreditation scheme, on the other hand, is in full swing, with a Code of Standards, a logo for landlords (along the lines of a kite mark) and plenty of help and support from the council (www.salford.gov.uk. Type 'landlord accreditation scheme' in the search box). The same goes for Wokingham (www.wokingham.gov.uk), who have also arranged special discounts for accredited landlords.

Some important considerations

Before you let your property you must make sure that you have the right to do so, and that your insurance company is aware of what you are doing. Please read on.

Are you allowed?

Before letting your property, you must make sure you actually have the right to do so.

Mortgaged property

Is your property mortgaged? If so, it will be a condition of your mortgage – unless, of course, you are buying it on a **buy-to-let mortgage** (see Chapter 6), in which case your lender will already have 'blessed' your plans – to obtain your bank/building society's consent to any letting. In practice, they are unlikely to mind as long as the letting is on an **assured shorthold tenancy** (see below).

If you tell your mortgage lender, the good news is that they will 'bless' the arrangement. The bad news is that they will almost certainly charge you up to £100 for (alleged) administrative expenses. They may also decide to put up your interest rate. You may well have to pay up because they will just add it to the amount you already owe them. However, before agreeing to pay extra interest, check to see that they really have the right to do this to you.

We cannot advise you to deceive your mortgage lender or breach the terms of the mortgage, but you might want to think carefully before telling them your plans. Unlike your insurers, they may not really *need* to know, and your honesty may cost you dear (see above). This is something you must decide for yourself.

Leasehold property

Almost all flats and some houses are **leasehold**, which means that you own the lease but pay **ground rent** to the owner of the site on which the property stands. If your property is leasehold, you will usually need the consent of your landlord (the person or organisation to whom you pay ground rent) to **sub-let**. You should not be charged for this but the landlord can pass on any costs incurred, such as for having your Tenancy Agreement checked.

The normal arrangement is for you to continue to pay standing charges such as ground rent and buildings insurance. Set your rent at a level which covers these.

If you are thinking of buying leasehold property to let, do make sure that there isn't an absolute ban on sub-letting!

Are you insured?

Your insurance company will want to know what you are up to. Tell them in writing and keep a copy (you will find a sample letter on p 128 of this book and on our website). *Don't let your property until you have your insurers' go-ahead.*

If you do not tell your insurance company, they may be able to refuse to pay out on a claim such as for a fire caused by your tenant's negligence.

Many contents insurance policies have in their small print a get-out clause which means you will not be compensated for theft from your property unless entry has been forced. The insurance company may therefore be able to avoid paying out in the event of theft by your tenant (who, of course, has a key!).

A tenant in Felixstowe recently did a moonlight flit, taking the entire contents of the property with him. The landlord's insurers refused to pay out.

You will also need insurance against claims which may arise if your tenants are injured as a result of defects in your property or contents.

1   We hope that everything will go well for you, but in case it doesn't you would be wise to have legal expenses cover. Many household policies include legal expenses cover as a matter of course – check yours.

2   Make friends with the Small Landlords' Association (SLA), an organisation which is run by small landlords for small landlords. The SLA offer members their own insurance scheme. They say, 'For many members the savings compared to their previous insurer save their SLA subscription several times over'. Their scheme covers situations many insurers would reject out of hand, such as landlords who rent to asylum seekers (for details, see 'Useful contacts').

You are not tied to the SLA for your insurance, however. There are bewildering numbers of insurance companies offering supposedly advantageous deals for landlords. Start with www.quote4mortgages.com and click on 'Are you paying too much ...' at the bottom of the home page.

6

Buy-to-let

If you are considering buying property, with or without a mortgage, with a view to renting it out – this chapter is for you.

What you are looking for is a good return on your money. Suppose property in your area is fetching low prices, while rents are fairly high. You look at a £50,000 house, which can command £6,000 a year in rent, and you wonder if this offers a better return for your money than a building society. However, if this means that the property is expensive to maintain, and if it is unlikely to attract reliable tenants, you may find that

o   you get a poor return on your money, and
o   the cost of borrowing makes the financial consequences even more severe for you.

Remember that borrowing money for investment has a 'gearing' effect, so if things go well they go very well, and if the investment underperforms the damage is magnified.

Suppose you are looking to buy in what is already an expensive area: you may find that the rental income provides only a small percentage return on your money. On the other hand, you may benefit from good quality tenants and, perhaps, property price rises. There again, house prices can and do go down as well as up. Although you can see the bricks and mortar, you are still speculating – and *if you have a buy-to-let mortgage you are taking chances with borrowed money.*

Or you might have a son or daughter going off to university or college in a town where lodgings are scarce and expensive, but house prices are fairly low. This consideration would normally rule out anywhere where property prices are high, such as Cambridge, but there may be bargains to be had in university towns with low house prices but high rental demand. You may decide to buy a property near the campus and rent it to a group of students, including your own offspring.

If you rent to students, make sure *you* are the landlord, not one of the tenants (your child, for example). It can be difficult for a young person to 'police' a property, keep the rents coming in and stay friends with their fellow occupants.

With any luck, you will be able to sell the house at a profit at the end of the three or four years. Many people have done this successfully. Bear in mind, however, that if the university town is a long way from where you live you may be unfamiliar with the area and you could get stung.

Raising the money

'Yes,' we hear you say, 'That's fine, but I'd need a mortgage.' Until recently, people like you were in for a hard time. Most people go to building societies for mortgages. Building societies exist primarily to enable people to buy their own homes, not to make a killing on the property market, and they are traditionally very unhappy about lending money on property to rent out. If a building society did offer a mortgage on such a property, it would set a higher rate of interest, demand large surcharges and very often refuse to take the rental income into account in assessing the borrower's ability to repay the loan.

New legislation, and an initiative by the Association of Rental Letting Agents (ARLA) (see 'Useful contacts'), changed that for ever. ARLA got together with several major lenders and launched the **Buy-to-Let** Scheme. Borrowers can get loans without paying higher interest rates or surcharges and the lender will usually take the potential rental income into account in calculating the borrower's ability to repay the loan.

Do your homework

Buy-to-let is not a get rich quick investment. You need to do your homework.

o How much would you have to pay for a suitable property?

o How much deposit would you have to pay up front?

o How much would you have to spend on doing it up?

o How much rent is it likely to command?

o What demand is there for rental property in that area?

o Can you afford to pay the mortgage if the property is empty for any length of time?

o Would the rent contribute sufficiently to the mortgage payments plus the maintenance, insurance, agent's fees and other outgoings?

Look for "buy to let" on the web; you will be offered hundreds of sites, notably those of letting agents anxious to manage your property for you.

Try also to talk to several landlords who have tried buy-to-let. *Then make up your own mind.*

Here, meanwhile, is a whistle-stop tour of the pros and cons of borrowing money to buy a rental property.

Pros

o You may get – in theory at least – a better return on your money than you would in a savings account.

o The rent will contribute to the mortgage payments.

o You can keep an eye on your investment – no sharp young men in red braces can gamble with it.

o You can set the interest off against rent when calculating your profit for tax purposes.

o If property prices rise you are on to a good thing.

o There is a choice of fixed-rate or flexible mortgages to suit differing needs.

Cons

o   Few buy-to-let mortgage lenders will advance more than 80% of a property's value.

o   You carry on paying off your mortgage even when the property is sitting empty.

o   If you're getting on a bit you may have trouble borrowing the money over more than five or 10 years.

o   A good slice of your rental income may well go on paying a managing agent (many lenders insist that you instruct one).

o   Property values can go down as well as up and you might find yourself owing more than your property is worth (the buzzword here is *negative equity* and it is *bad news*).

o   Rents can go down as well as up.

o   So can demand for rental property.

o   You may – especially if your rental income is more than £15,000 a year – find yourself being charged tax on rent arrears, that is, rents which have become payable but which you have not yet received. If you never get the rent you can claim bad debt relief, but you are out of pocket in the meantime (see Chapter 16).

Can you afford to keep up the payments even if you don't get any rent? The Small Landlords Association reckons that as many as one letting in 20 results in disputes between landlord and tenant; and however easy getting shot of a bad tenant may seem in theory, there is always hassle involved. Little has changed since Shakespeare talked of 'the law's delay' and you could find yourself with a tenant who owes three months' rent and is clocking up arrears like a taxi meter while the local court seems unable to appreciate the urgency of your case. Meanwhile, you are servicing a big loan on property which is not bringing in a penny.

PART 2
FINDING A TENANT

7

Do you need an agent?

You can go it alone, or you can call in a letting agent – someone whose business it is to manage other people's property. Many high street estate agents let property as well as selling it, but some agents specialise in letting only.

Going it alone is either free or fairly cheap, and you get tax relief (see Chapter 16) on the cost of any advertising. The down-side is that you are on your own. Nobody is going to select your tenant, collect the rent for you, argue with a bad tenant or help you if things go wrong. If this worries you, consider using an agent.

Inexperienced landlords often find it helpful to instruct an agent for their first let, then strike out on their own when they feel more confident.

What will a letting agent do for you?

Good agents will:
o   find a suitable tenant, while leaving the final choice up to you;
o   prepare and complete the Tenancy Agreement.

If your agents want to use their own Tenancy Agreement, check theirs against the one in this book to make sure it protects your interests.

An agent should also be able to:

o   advise you on how much rent you should be
     charging;

o   advise you about any refurbishment, repairs, etc
     that should be done before letting (a little work
     now could mean an extra £100 a month later);

o   hold any deposit in a separate account (that is, *not*
     mixed up with the agents' own money) from which
     you get the interest;

o   collect the rent and pass it on to you at once;

o   keep proper records of money paid out and
     received;

o   inspect the property regularly and let you know if
     anything needs attention;

o   take all necessary steps to obtain vacant possession
     of the property when the letting ends;

o   charge only a reasonable commission – that is, not
     more than 12.5%–15% of rent paid plus VAT. Note
     that many agents charge their tenants too. If this
     bothers you, ask for details of their practices;

o   have professional indemnity insurance so that you
     can be compensated if mistakes are made.

Having said this, we should mention that many agents
offer several levels of service. Typically they are:

o   Introduction only (sometimes called *let and vet*):
     –   finding a tenant;
     –   taking up references;
     –   preparing the Tenancy Agreement (check to
          make sure it's the same as ours – see the Power
          point above);
     –   preparing the inventory and getting it signed;
     –   collecting deposit and first month's rent.

     After that you're on your own. Expect to pay a flat
     fee.

o   Rent collection service:
     –   all the above plus regular collection of rent.
          They might charge a flat fee, or a percentage of
          the rent.

o   Full management:
  –   all the above, plus all the day to day
      management: repairs, inspections, notices to
      quit, etc. This is the one you would probably
      want if you were going to be out of the
      country.

Do your homework

Before you decide on a particular agent, do your homework. Access the ARLA website and download all the free literature you can conveniently digest (there is an awful lot of it). Then either use ARLA to find likely-looking agents in your area or buy your local newspaper on the day that covers property and note the details of all the letting agents.

Most agents will be happy to put you in touch with satisfied clients, but keep your eyes and ears open for other sources of information – word gets around. Meanwhile, here are the pros and cons of instructing an agent.

Advantage: an agent can do everything for you: this is helpful if, for example, you are letting your home while you are working abroad.

Disadvantage: this is going to cost money (although you can set the agent's fees against tax). How much depends on the individual agent. Also, you are handing over control to someone else – and there are plenty of incompetent agents around (see below).

The rogue agent

Anybody can set themselves up as a letting agent without any qualifications or experience, and some do. Some are merely incompetent, but there are also rogue agents who collect rents and deposits from tenants and fail either to pass on the rents to the landlords or to return the deposits to the tenants. When a letting agent in Newmarket bankrupted herself without warning, the list of creditors (people to whom she owed money) was 12 pages long, and nobody ever found any of the money.

All those landlords lost large sums in rent, and were also legally responsible for returning the deposits to the tenants. This may seem unfair, especially as the landlords never saw the money in the first place, but it's the law. The rogue agent was prosecuted and found guilty. She did probation and the last time we heard of her she was working for a letting agent!

A good starting point in your search for a reliable agent is the Association of Residential Letting Agents (ARLA). Contact them either by telephone or through their website (details in 'Useful contacts'). All ARLA agents must carry professional indemnity insurance and operate separate client bank accounts.

8

Set your stall out

Before you start actively hunting for a tenant for yourself or instructing an agent to do so, you need to look carefully at the property you are offering. A lot of landlords forget that they are promoting a product – their property – and that good tenants are apt to be choosy.

Quite apart from being habitable, safe and in good repair, your property needs to be attractive. Here are some pointers.

o   Decorate in pale, neutral colours for maximum light and freshness.

o   Either have an agreement with your tenant ('You may put up pictures and posters provided you make good with filler and paint before you leave'), or put up some wooden picture rails from a DIY shop to enable your tenant to put up pictures without damaging your walls.

o   Good quality paint lasts longer than wallpaper and is easier and quicker to renew.

o   Durable, good quality carpets and curtains are essential, especially in an unfurnished property where they are not hidden by furniture. Cheap carpet is a bad buy. Your mantra here is *bombproof* – heavy domestic cords and Berber twists in neutral shades are very durable. Have them fitted by a reputable person and get a guarantee.

o   Kitchens need reliable appliances which are simple to operate (remember they are *your* responsibility if they go wrong).

o   If you are letting furnished property, pay particular attention to the safety regulations for upholstered furniture (see Chapter 3).

- Offer plenty of storage space. Consider installing fitted wardrobes in bedrooms, and in furnished property beds with drawers underneath are a good idea.
- Bathrooms and lavatories need to have extractor fans, good lighting and quality fittings, and tiles should be freshly grouted. Grubby grout is off-putting, and avocado baths are passé!
- A shower is essential – and so is a non-slip surface to stand on.

1 Go round the charity shops armed with your window measurements. People get tired of their curtains long before they wear out. You may pick up some treasures for a few pounds, then spend on carpets the money you have saved on curtains.

2 The small ads are a rich source of nearly-new bathroom fittings – £50 for a white bathroom suite with taps and waste is not unusual.

3 Revamping a kitchen need not cost a fortune. You can often spot complete two-year-old kitchens in the small ads for £100 or less, discarded in their owners' frantic efforts to keep up with the Joneses. Add some new worktops (second-hand ones are rarely the right size) and you've saved yourself a four-figure sum.

Track down a tenant

If you instruct an agent, they should find your tenant for you. If you are going it alone, you will need to do this yourself. The first step is:

Spreading the word

Ways of finding a tenant include:

o   word of mouth (but beware of letting to friends or relations – see below);

o   advertisements in newspapers or magazines read by the kind of person you hope to attract (see below). *Loot* is a particularly good classified paper (www.loot.com);

o   cards in shop windows;

o   noticeboards in supermarket foyers.

Beware!

Forget the clichés – there are exceptions to every rule except one. *Be wary of letting property to friends or relations!* You, of course, will know the individuals better than we do, but ask yourself:

o   Can I put the transaction on a businesslike footing and keep it that way?

o   Can I be as firm with them as with a stranger, such as in insisting on regular rent payments and observance of rules?

o   Can I be sure of getting rid of them when the time comes?

Unless the answer to all three questions is a resounding *yes*, find a good excuse for turning them down without hurting their feelings.

1   If you have a particular hobby or interest, you could consider advertising your property in a magazine aimed at that group of people. You might attract a fellow radio amateur/ biker/euphonium player that way.

2   Many advertising papers are delivered free to all the homes in a particular area. Get hold of a few, ask how much they charge for a small ad, and try your luck.

3   If you go for the shop window or notice board approach, a typed notice is better than a handwritten one. Remember, it's your first contact with prospective tenants: make it legible and attractive – *and omit your address* (see below).

Other sources

Why not consider the following:

University or college

The accommodation officers may be willing to pass on a handout of your details.

Some universities or colleges inspect prospective rental properties before they put you on their list, others are simply glad of another address to hand out to students.

Make sure you know who your tenant is! If you find yourself letting to the college housing office, this may amount to a 'company let'. This is not necessarily a bad thing, but it won't be an **assured shorthold tenancy** as we know it (for details see below).

Try, if you can, to liaise with the parents (who could, for example, come up with the deposit and then put pressure on the young people to behave!) rather than their offspring. In any case, get all the students' names on the tenancy agreement to make sure they are **jointly and severally** liable for the rent and for any damage.

Hospitals

There never seems to be enough accommodation for nurses and doctors and, as with universities and colleges, there will probably be an official who will be glad to add you to their database. The same considerations apply as to universities and colleges (see above).

Employers

Personnel departments of big employers in your area will usually be delighted to put you on their database or display a card on their notice board. Many will want short lets for employees who are new to the area or on fixed term contracts. Industries with highly mobile workforces are a prime target.

Company lets

By a 'company let', we mean one where your tenant is the company, not the individual. Many organisations like to have a pool of suitable rental property for their employees.

If you do let to a company, the tenancy agreement will not be an **assured shorthold tenancy**, which is for individuals only. In practice, the main difference between an assured shorthold tenancy and a company let will be that under the former, sub-letting (that is, by the tenant to a third party) is usually prohibited, whereas under the latter, sub-letting must be allowed – but controlled so that the sub-tenant (the employee) does not get the statutory right to stay in your property indefinitely. The Tenancy Agreement in this book *is not* a company letting agreement, and you should take professional advice.

There are, however, advantages to company lets.

o   A company might well be financially sounder than an individual (though it depends on the company – see below).

o   Rent may be paid in three- or six-month chunks in advance.

o   Companies often want long term lets for their staff and can offer you more continuity than some tenants can.

Possible snags are:

o   the company might want to use their own rental agreement. If so, take legal advice if it differs significantly from our Tenancy Agreement;

o   for the legal exemptions to apply you must be dealing with a company – not a private individual or a partnership;

o   a foreign company (that is, one not registered in the UK) could be a great nuisance if you need to claim for damage or unpaid rent.

Some companies are household names, but others may not be known to you. You can check them out instantly by doing a search on the Companies House website (see 'Useful contacts').

Planning your advertising

Advertisements in a local newspaper or magazine (national ones would probably cast your net too wide) can be expensive, but you do reach a larger readership than through shop windows, etc. Start by looking at other people's ads in the property section of your local newspaper and noting the accepted abbreviations that will save you money. Why pay for 'Gas fired central heating' if you can get away with 'GFCH'?

Small ads usually give all or most of the following information:

o   approximate location;

o   any obvious selling points (for example, 'quiet', 'newly dec', 'pte pkg', 'gdn' or 'nr shops');

o   rent expected, adding 'exc' if your tenant will be responsible for utility bills and 'inc' if they will not;

o   any special points (for example, 'Refs reqd', 'Quiet N/S prof' or 'Sorry no DSS');

o   contact telephone number, box number (see the Power point below) or possibly email address.

Draft an advertisement which seems OK to you – remember that this is your first contact with your potential tenant, so waste a word or two saying how attractive your property is. (Rosy started one ad for a smart modern studio with DROP DEAD GORGEOUS and received 37 replies!)

Your checklist:

o   Be brief – this is a small ad, not an estate agent's blurb (that comes later – see 'The blurb', below).

o   Be honest – don't say your property is immaculate if there are holes in the carpets and scuff marks on the walls. Prospective tenants will just blame you for wasting their time.

o   Be informative. Include all the relevant information. You are hoping to attract plenty of interest, but if you're advertising a town flat you don't want to waste time talking to people who are looking for a country cottage.

Then call the advertising department of your chosen publication and find out:

o   the deadline – if the property section of your local newspaper comes out on a Friday, you may need to submit your ad by Wednesday noon. Don't miss the boat;

o   the cost. Some tele-sales people are on commission and will try to sell you an elaborate package that you don't need, such as a free insertion if you pay for three. One insertion in the right place, at the right time, will usually be enough.

You may be able to dictate the ad over the telephone, paying by credit card. If so:

o   get them to send a copy of the invoice for your file – and keep it safe, because it's worth money to you in the form of tax relief;

o   spell out anything potentially confusing;

o   have the tele-sales person repeat the entire ad to you, especially the contact details. You can usually get a free insertion in the next issue if they goof seriously, such as getting your telephone number wrong, but their carelessness could lose you a week's rent.

When advertising in a newspaper or magazine, it is a good idea to use a box number if you are not in a tearing hurry. A box number costs a little extra but saves you fielding a lot of telephone calls at inconvenient times (see above!) and the newspaper or magazine will tell you how to set one up. We know of landlords who receive up to 50 enquiries from one ad; a box number allows some preliminary sifting before you start telephoning applicants.

Tenants receiving benefits

Sometimes you see something along the lines of 'Sorry no DSS' in property ads. This kind of discrimination has not been challenged in the courts – yet. For the moment you are free to choose whether or not to let to someone receiving benefits. Do not, however, close your mind to this possibility without considering the advantages and disadvantages.

One important advantage is free home improvements. A tenant receiving benefits may qualify you for some very valuable improvements to your property (see p 28 for details of Warm Front, the government's free home energy scheme). The only string attached is that you must promise not to raise the rent for a reasonable time – usually a year – after the improvements have been completed (see 'Useful contacts' for details).

Sources of supply

There are three likely sources of potential tenants in receipt of benefits:

o   replies to your own advertising;

o   your local authority Housing Department;

o   local homelessness charities and similar organisations.

Not all areas are well served by the homelessness charities. The national homelessness organisations, such as Shelter, tend to be better at giving legal advice than actually finding accommodation, but there are some wonderful local initiatives, often operating on a shoestring.

In the authors' own area, a Housing Action Group works hand in hand with the local authority and benefits agencies to match landlords with prospective lodgers and tenants.

Their relationship with landlords is exemplary. They will take careful note of the landlord's requirements and can often arrange for the landlord to meet several prospective tenants, all armed with references. They will lend a hand with form-filling for candidates on benefits and may even be able to provide deposits from their own funds or from related charities (who may be a good source of deposits). They can often advance the first month's rent too, which is a thing no local authority, however helpful otherwise, is likely to do (though see below about the 'deposit guarantee scheme').

Some of these organisations will themselves rent your property and then **sub-let** it to people on their books. The advantages for you, the landlord, are that the organisation will usually agree terms by which:

o   the rent is paid in full and on time, whether the property is occupied or empty;

o   they are liable for any damage or loss (while the actual occupant might do a flit, the organisation is always accessible).

Just make sure that any agreement you sign with them achieves these objectives. If in doubt, take professional advice.

Potential tenants don't need to be claiming benefits to consult a Housing Action Group – many people in good jobs who are new to the area approach the group rather than an agent, who may charge them extortionate fees for poor service.

To see what your local housing action group equivalent is, approach your local Citizens Advice Bureau for details of organisations operating in your area.

Direct payment of rent

If you do take a tenant who qualifies for housing benefit, you can (with the tenant's agreement – there is a special form for you both to sign) arrange for the rent to be paid directly to you. If a tenant receiving housing benefit gets behind with the rent, the housing authority can choose to pay you direct anyway, but as there usually have to be at least eight weeks' arrears before the arrangement kicks in, you may prefer to be paid direct from the beginning.

Housing benefit

Housing benefit is paid by local councils to people claiming benefits or on low incomes to help them to pay their rent. The system is quite complex and ponderously bureaucratic (but see 'Hold the front page!' below). The amount of housing benefit the authorities will pay out for a particular tenant is based on:

o   the tenant's income and capital (for example, savings);

o   the tenant's age and personal circumstances;

o   the amount of rent the tenant will have to pay;

o   whether this rent includes any other charges, such as utilities (if so, their housing benefit will be reduced accordingly);

o   the tenant's housing need;

o   what the local Rent Service regards as the going rate for the accommodation you are offering (this may not be the same as what the private market will bear).

The *extent* of the accommodation (quite apart from the level of rent) your prospective tenant is entitled to depends on the tenant's age and circumstances: a single person under 25 would rate one room with shared facilities, a couple with a child would qualify for two bedrooms, and so on. The housing department of the local authority will decide what accommodation the tenant is entitled to. Most local authorities publish helpful leaflets setting out exactly what each individual or family group is entitled to, or you can access the Shelternet website (see 'Useful contacts').

The housing department then asks the Rent Service to assess what is called a 'local reference rent' for the property. In theory, you can expect an official with a clipboard to knock on the door of your property and ask to inspect it. In practice, the 'inspection' may simply be done in the office, based on a glance at the street map of your area and the rent officer's knowledge of the going rate for the kind of property you are offering. If the rent you are asking coincides with the local reference rent as well as with the tenant's other benefit entitlements, the housing benefit will cover the rent in full.

1   Your prospective tenant can find out in advance whether their housing benefit entitlement will cover the rent you are charging by asking the local housing department for a Pre Tenancy Determination before moving in. Application forms are obtainable from local council offices.

2   There is (see above) no point in choosing a tenant whose circumstances and housing need do not coincide with the size and rent of the property you are letting. The local authority will only pay housing benefit to match the tenant's housing need. *You* cannot apply for a Pre-Tenancy Determination – the tenant has to do that – but you can, before you start interviewing, find out from your local authority or the Shelternet site (see 'Useful contacts') what types of tenant or family group will rate the accommodation you are offering.

If the rent you are charging is higher than the tenant's housing benefit entitlement, you will have to collect the excess from the tenant. Ask yourself – how likely is it that a tenant receiving benefits will be able to pay this?

Be patient

You may face a longish wait for your money while your case works its way laboriously through the local authority system. This is where the 'rent advance scheme' offered by some homeless charities could come into its own. Ask about this.

If a tenant claiming benefits is unable to offer you a deposit, don't despair. Many local authorities run 'deposit guarantee schemes' (see below).

Coping with officialdom

This is not intended as a diatribe against local authorities, who for the most part do their best, but it is worth mentioning that officials can and do mislay documents and then deny ever having received them. This is often due to the 'If I can't find it on the computer system it doesn't exist' phenomenon. It can take many working days to transfer the information from a stack of forms onto the computer system and forms have been known to go AWOL before their details have been entered, and people can and do make typing errors in transferring information onto their database. Of course, the inconvenience for you is the same whatever the reason for the hiccup. In your dealings with officialdom it pays to:

o   open a file labelled with the address of your rental property;

o   make a note of any reference number or code allocated to your case. Write this in thick black felt tip on the file, and quote it in every communication – both by telephone and in writing – with the authority;

o   keep a copy of everything you send or hand in;

o   keep careful notes for your file of all telephone conversations, with dates and the name of the official you spoke to. You think you will remember, but in a month's time you will have forgotten all about it;

o   get a signed receipt for everything you hand in and never, ever part with it until you have taken a copy;

o   make friends with an official connected with your case, write their name and telephone extension number on the front of the file in thick black felt tip and call them regularly to ask about progress.

Clawing back overpayments

Having your tenant's housing benefit paid straight to you can work very well. You get the money before your tenant can spend it on riotous living or shoes for the children, but beware! If, because of your tenant's benefit fraud, the local authority pays out more money than the tenant is entitled to – *even if you yourself are totally unaware of anything untoward* – the local authority will claw back the overpayment from you. You have to sign a form agreeing to this, and every few months your local authority will enclose a reminder about it with your regular statement, so you cannot plead ignorance.

They have the **statutory** power to recover this money from you and, because they are generously rewarded by central government for doing so, they will do their utmost to exercise that power.

They will do it either by

o   demanding payment from *you* there and then, *or*

o   deducting the overpayment in instalments from the ongoing rent.

Either way is bad news. If you don't pay, local authorities have the power to take you to court for the money, and recent case law indicates that they will win. A county court judgment (see below) against you would affect your future credit rating. It sure as hell ain't fair on an innocent landlord, but that is what will happen!

You are then supposed to claim the money back from your tenant, but this is stressful at best and costly at worst. Suppose you buy *Debt Recovery* in this series and use it to get a county court judgment against your tenant. This is quite straightforward – but you may never see your money. You can't get blood out of a stone! The judge will take the tenant's income into account and may order them to pay off their debt in such small instalments that you might as well have written off the money in the first place. This is, of course, a worst-case scenario, and if you choose your tenant carefully it may never happen to you.

The poverty trap

Many landlords have problems with tenants who, after a time on benefits, find work and receive a pay cheque instead of a benefit giro. You might think this would be good news for everyone, and of course in many ways it is, but many tenants have trouble making ends meet because they do not realise that financial help is available. It is in your interests as a landlord that your tenant claims everything they are entitled to.

A new system for family support started in April 2003. It is called 'child tax credit' and 'working tax credit'. The government has claimed this as 'the biggest revolution in the tax and benefits system since Beveridge'.

Child tax credit replaces allowances given for children previously incorporated within income support, working family tax credit, job seeker's allowance, the former children's tax credit and disabled person's tax credit. Under legislative provision contained in the Tax Credits Act 2002, child tax credit is now available to persons who are responsible for at least one child, or a 'qualifying young person' – for example, an individual under the age of 19 and still in full time education, but not in advanced education, such as university. Child tax credit is also available in respect of a young person who has not yet reached the age of 18, but who has registered for work or training and has not been in full time education for a consecutive period of 20 weeks.

Working tax credit is available to people aged 16 or over, in paid employment for 16 hours a week and responsible for at least one child, or who are disabled, or those who are aged 25 or over and normally work for at least 30 hours per week.

There are complex formulas for calculating the amount of child tax credit and working tax credit, but if your tenant thinks they may be eligible for either or both of these tax credits they can get more detail and order application forms from the Inland Revenue's website (see 'Useful contacts').

Your tenant may also be able to claim *council tax benefit* and, of course, if your tenant has children and their other parent is living elsewhere, the tenant may be able to claim child support through the Child Support Agency. It is commoner for mothers to claim, but fathers can too.

Even after claiming all the benefits they are entitled to, a *working* tenant may qualify for less housing benefit and council tax benefit, not to mention possibly losing free school meals, free prescriptions and other goodies that people on benefits receive. There are schemes to cushion the blow – the tenant can usually get some extra housing benefit to tide them over until the first pay cheque arrives.

Hold the front page!

At the time of writing, the housing benefit system is under review. The government is getting ready to pilot a new system called the 'standard local housing allowance' which, in theory at least, will do away with the bureaucracy of the current system.

The idea is to have a set amount of money available in each area for housing costs, according to the size of the family. So a single person would be entitled to X, a couple to Y, a couple with a child to Z, and so on. The claimant would then know in advance how much money they were entitled to, and could look for accommodation at around that price. If they could find something for less money, they would be allowed to keep the difference; if the accommodation was more expensive, they would have to make up the difference.

If all goes well, the government will bring in legislation to change the whole housing benefit system. The buzzword is Pathfinder, and the new system is being piloted in 10 different areas, from October 2003–April 2004.

One important change which affects you, the landlord, is that under the new scheme the tenant will not have the option of having their benefit paid direct to the landlord unless the tenant is either very vulnerable or has more than eight weeks' rent arrears.

The selection process

The two authors of this book see eye to eye about most things, but they could not agree about strategies for selecting a tenant. Mark is a hard-headed property lawyer, but has never rented out property himself. He favours an objective approach, drawing up a list of headings and awarding points for each one. So a prospective tenant might rate five points for having a steady job and another five for having good references, but lose two points for being a smoker – and so on.

Rosy, who owns and manages seven properties and rarely has any problems, likes his approach very much, but her selection process will always include an element of intuition and gut reaction as well.

We would not presume to tell *you* how to choose a tenant, but the points below – which include both approaches – are worth taking into consideration.

First, however, a word of warning!

Be on your guard

Your prospective tenants are complete strangers. Most people are harmless, but statistically you are bound to come across some doubtful characters eventually. To protect yourself, consider some or all of the following points when fielding phone calls (or, indeed, opt for a box number – see the Power point on p 52).

- Be aware that not all callers may be looking for accommodation, and that some villains can be very plausible.

- Don't give your full address in any advertisement – a contact telephone number is enough.

- When someone rings to enquire about your property, write down whatever telephone number they give you, then ring 1471 afterwards to check that the two numbers are the same. There may be a good reason for any discrepancy – but on the other hand, there may not.

- Avoid giving any personal information – such as the fact that you live alone – in your advertisement or on the telephone.

- Don't answer late-night telephone calls. People can call again at a reasonable hour, or forget the whole thing.

- If the call turns obscene or malicious, resist the temptation to burst into tears (they'll love it) or make wisecracks (they'll call you again to see if you can keep it up). Just put down the receiver, do a swift 1471 in case they've been careless, and if you feel it is justified, tell both your telephone company and the police.

- Don't give a candidate the address of the property until you are sure you want to meet them.

- Before meeting a candidate, always call them at home or at work, ostensibly to confirm the time of your appointment, but in reality to check that the contact information they gave you is correct.

- Listen to your inner voice. If you don't like the sound of them, don't meet them face to face.

Telephone vetting

Be near the telephone, armed with pen and paper, as soon as your ad appears – and that can mean as early as 7 am. In many localities, an attractively worded 'To Let' ad brings in at least 20 enquiries.

Unless you are using a box number, make sure you are at home on the day your ad appears. Many people are nervous of answering machines and ring off without leaving a message, and you could lose the ideal tenant that way.

The first telephone contact gives you an opportunity of checking your prospective tenants unobtrusively. Do remember, however, that your potential tenants will be checking you out too!

You are looking for someone who will:

o   pay the rent;

o   take care of your property;

o   be a considerate neighbour.

This person is going to live in your property and you have every right to turn down anyone you find uncongenial or who you think might cause annoyance to you or your neighbours (but see 'Beware discrimination', below).

Three questions you may be asked

o   **Do you accept children?**

    You can, of course, decide what line you are going to take, and stick to it. If you cherish your soft furnishings, or if the property itself is not very child-friendly (a third floor flat with nowhere to park a pram), say so.

o   **Do you accept pets?**

    If you hate the thought of dog or cat hairs and worse on your carpets, or if you are offering a top floor flat, say firmly 'Sorry, no pets' and hang on until someone comes along who shares your views. Keep an open mind about less troublesome pets – a total ban on goldfish, stick insects and budgies could be construed as unreasonable under the terms of the OFT guidelines (see p 105) and could lose you a good tenant.

o   **Are people receiving benefits welcome?** (for the pros and cons of this, see Chapter 10).

If you hate the idea of someone on income support or jobseeker's allowance in your property, stick to your guns. It isn't against the law – yet.

Another way of handling these questions is to keep your options open. Say cautiously, 'It depends on the individual children/pets/people', see the people, children and pets for yourself and use your common sense.

Be meticulous

Sift candidates as you talk on the telephone, making notes to keep on file.

Use a fresh sheet of paper for each caller. It is surprisingly easy to mislay people's details unless you are organised. That is why the checklist opposite will be helpful.

You may find yourself rejecting several hopefuls before you actually make an appointment to show anyone around. This is to be expected.

Be safe!

When you do make an appointment to meet them, ask the prospective tenant to bring along a photo ID (driving licence, work ID, passport) with them. That way you will be able to verify basic information about the applicant's identity, and will discourage imposters!

Checklist: first telephone contact with prospective tenant

[Consider printing out several of these]

Candidate's name ....

Where do they come from? ....

Contact telephone number ....

At work   ❏

Student   ❏

On benefits   ❏

Can they give references?   ❏

Deposit available?   ❏

Any other information they offer about themselves ....

....

....

Arrange to show around   ❏

Date ....

Time ....

Put on backup list   ❏

Not suitable   ❏

The blurb

This is a typed description of your property to hand, post, email or fax to prospective tenants who have survived the first sift. Include such information as:

o   your name and a contact telephone number;

o   the exact address of the property;

o   directions for getting there if it is likely to be a problem;

o   distances from shops, public transport;

o   anything else you think is likely to be useful – for example, prospective tenants of a family house will want to know about schools, while an elderly person will want to know how far away the shops are;

o   a brief description of the accommodation;

o   how much council tax is payable (see below);

o   what utilities are available and who pays for them (for example, is the water supply metered? Is the gas/electric on a card meter?);

o   the monthly rent;

o   the deposit.

The blurb gives short-listed candidates the necessary information in a handy, user-friendly form and saves you answering a great many questions many times over. It also makes sure they don't mislay your contact details.

Once you have drafted your blurb, keep it on file or even better, on disk, for future use. Remember, you may need to update it from time to time.

Face to face

You will probably have to set half a day or so aside for showing people round and interviewing them.

Remember – you don't know these people. All you know about them is what they have told you themselves. If you are haunted by the fate of estate agent Suzy Lamplugh, who left the office to show a client called Mr Kipper round a property and was never seen again, nobody can blame you for being cautious.

1   If you have not done much interviewing or showing-round before, consider having a dry run with a friend playing the part of a prospective tenant.

2   Try to arrange for a friend or, if you have one, your dog to be with you when you do meet candidates. Your friend can check out the candidates and help you by taking notes, and if your normally benign hound growls and goes all stiff-legged, ask yourself why.

3   Allow plenty of time for each prospective tenant. Half an hour is about right. It should give you enough time to show the prospective tenant round and interview them as you go, plus a few minutes to make notes after they've left.

4   Always take notes. As any experienced interviewer will tell you, interviewees seem to merge into each other after the first half dozen or so.

5   Be prepared for the occasional 'no show'. A spare half hour is no bad thing; you can use the time to bring your notes on the other candidates up to date.

6   Remember, yours will not be the only property on the candidates' list. People can and do drop out. Don't stop noting names and telephone numbers and don't stop interviewing over the telephone, even if you think you have the perfect tenant plus a couple of spares.

7   Keep a record of suitable tenants who didn't quite make it first time around. Then, next time you have a property vacant, you can call them and maybe save yourself the cost of a newspaper advert and a lot of interviewing.

When each candidate arrives

Have their first contact details in front of you and a list of points to mention (council tax? TV licence?). Check the photo ID which (see above) you have asked them to bring with them.

Give them your blurb if you have not already sent a copy (see above).

Try to envisage the kinds of questions you are likely to be asked (see above), and have your answers ready.

Here are some points to consider.

o   Are you prepared to accept a tenant in receipt of benefits (see Chapter 10)? If not, are you satisfied that your prospective tenant will be able to pay the rent? We're not talking about demanding a detailed statement of their income and expenditure here, just some indication that there is enough money coming in from a reliable source.

o   Has your prospective tenant got either the deposit or the means to obtain it (there are schemes to help housing benefit clients with deposits)?

o   Does your prospective tenant seem clean, tidy and punctual? We would reject out of hand anyone who turned up late for their interview without a good reason, wearing anything other than clean clothes and 'shining morning face'. This is, of course, a matter of personal preference and you are welcome to disagree.

o   Is your prospective tenant being frank with you? Beware of anyone who seems unwilling to talk about their employer, their previous landlord, etc. You will, of course, in any case ask for references – and follow them up (see 'References', below).

o   If you have firm views on smoking, pets, etc, that's fine: stick to your guns. However, many landlords prefer to look at each individual smoker or pet owner on their merits (see above).

o   Is there anything about the prospective tenant that might annoy you or your neighbours? Someone intent on keeping several dogs or learning the saxophone is unlikely to be popular.

Be business-like, but listen to your own gut reactions too. If there seems something faintly suspect about a prospective tenant, something you can't quite put your finger on, there is probably a good reason. Trust your intuition. You will not often be wrong.

Be patient. Shyness and nervousness are no indication of a bad tenant.

They're checking you out too

Remember that while you are cautiously assessing your prospective tenant, *you* are being checked out too. Be punctual and make sure both you and the property look clean and presentable.

Some candidates may have several places to view. Make sure you hand out copies of your blurb (see above) to remind them what you are offering.

Accepting and rejecting

Never decide on the spot, however strong your gut feeling about someone. Say 'I'll let you know', name a day or time to call them, and keep your promise. Then use the time to follow up references.

Beware discrimination

Racial discrimination is against the law. Even if you draft a racially discriminatory ad, no responsible newspaper will publish it.

You must not turn away a prospective tenant on grounds of race or colour. Apart from the fact that you might be turning down the perfect tenant, you could be committing a criminal offence.

o   Sex discrimination is also unlawful (but see exceptions below).

o   Discrimination on grounds of sexual orientation is not unlawful – yet, but only because the UK has so far failed to implement Article 13 of the Treaty of Amsterdam.

Sex discrimination is allowed in the provision of hostel-style accommodation, where for reasons of decency and propriety 'mixed bathing' is prohibited. Similarly, if you are letting a room in your own home you can also choose the sex of your lodger.

- 'No DSS' is not (yet) unlawful, even though it may, by implication, discriminate against people from ethnic minorities and, for example, single parents.
- The Disability Discrimination Act 1995 makes it unlawful to discriminate against a disabled person because of their disability. Disability, in this context, includes mental as well as physical impairment.

The Act applies specifically to residential property – so as landlord you cannot turn someone down because of disability, or offer them less favourable terms (for example, higher rent) than other candidates. Moreover, if the disabled person sues you, the burden of proof is on you to show that you did not treat the disabled person less favourably because of their disability. (You can, of course, still reject a disabled candidate for some other, unrelated reason – such as bad references or inability to look after the property in accordance with the terms of the Tenancy Agreement.)

However, you are not under an obligation to let to a disabled person accommodation that presents them with a health and safety risk. Nor do you have to let to someone without the mental capacity to enter into a binding contract. The Act does not apply to small owner-occupied premises – which basically exempts people taking in lodgers.

Be nice

In turning somebody down, be kind and tactful. Nobody likes to feel rejected. Emphasise how difficult it was to make your choice. Word gets around. The unsuccessful candidates will inevitably talk to their friends and colleagues, and you would prefer them to speak well of you.

1   When you call your chosen tenant to inform them of their good fortune, *tell them that the deal is subject to satisfactory references* (see Chapter 12).

2   Try not to worry about possible loss of income if you are slow in establishing your tenant. It is better to have a lean couple of weeks while you seek out the perfect tenant than to install one in haste and regret it at leisure.

References and deposits

Once you have made your choice, it is time to do some serious checking. However charming your prospective tenant seems, the two key questions are always:

o   Can your tenant pay the rent?

o   Will your tenant look after your property?

Nothing can guarantee a 'yes' to both questions, but you can reduce the risks by:

o   asking for references;

o   following them up;

o   taking a deposit (see below).

Do not rely on references which the tenant hands you. As an example of what might happen, a colleague once interviewed a prospective tenant whose glowing testimonial, supposedly from their employer, turned out to be bogus. Well, to be precise, the headed paper was genuine, the tenant was who he said he was, but when our colleague telephoned the firm, she found that the man had been sacked for dishonesty the week before and had typed the document himself. If our colleague had been lax about checking him out, she could have let her property to a cheat.

Always look for:

o   a financial reference, such as from an employer, if appropriate (is their job secure?);

o   a reference from a previous landlord (why did they leave?);

o   a personal reference from a responsible person who has known them for at least three years.

Take up the references. You can find a sample request for a reference on p 129.

Some referees will be more forthcoming over the telephone than in a letter – listen carefully and note any hesitation or too-careful choice of words. Many people are reluctant to speak ill of anyone, but there are ways of leaving things unsaid.

Serious checking

We know another landlord who was defrauded by a tenant with immaculate references from both his employer and his bank. However, if the landlord had checked more thoroughly he would have thought twice about granting him a tenancy. This man had recently arrived in the area and opened a new bank account, but he had county court judgments against him in another part of the country and his creditworthiness was nil.

Much financial information about people is confidential, and is jealously guarded by the Data Protection Act 1998. There are, however, sources of information which are publicly accessible:

o   the Register of County Court Judgments (see 'Useful contacts') – this costs £4;

but this register does not include High Court judgments (which do not figure on any register), so really big debts can go unrecorded.

o   the Individual Insolvency Register (see 'Useful contacts') keeps details of bankruptcy and individual voluntary arrangements (a sort of half-way house between solvency and insolvency) and does not charge;

o   credit reference agencies – these use 'credit scoring systems' and then allocate a pass mark to predict whether or not people are a good credit risk.

An example of an online service is Experian, which offers a Tenant Verifier Service (see 'Useful contacts'). This service 'specialises in providing detailed financial and rental history checks on prospective tenants in order to identify the financial risk'. Access their website and click on 'Prices' to see how much it will cost to use their services. Many letting agents and major landlords have accounts with this service. There are some useful FAQs on their site, which you can access for free.

If online credit references are not your scene, there are plenty of conventional ones. See Yellow Pages for your local agencies, or call Talking Pages on 0800 600 900 for a free, nationwide trawl.

Using a credit reference agency will, of course, cost you and it may not be totally reliable.

Deposits

Many landlords ask prospective tenants for a substantial deposit in addition to the first month's rent. There is no upper or lower limit set by law, but one or two months' rent would be normal. This sum can be used to cover any unpaid rent, to pay the cost of cleaning the property when the tenant leaves and to make good any damage they have done. The deposit (or what is left after such deductions) should be returned to the tenant at the end of the letting period.

Deposits for tenants receiving state benefits

You may think that deposits would be out of the question for tenants on state benefits, but you would be wrong.

Many local authorities run a 'deposit guarantee scheme' for lodgers and tenants on benefits. Typically, the local authority gives the landlord a guarantee or bond (not actual money – see below) to cover a maximum of one month's rent. The bond is handed to the landlord as a deposit. In return for this, the lodger pays a small sum – typically £5 or £10 – to the local authority and promises:

o   to pay the rent promptly;

o   not to cause any damage;

o   to pay the Council for any damage that is caused.

If there is any damage at the end of the tenant's stay, the local authority – not the tenant – pays the landlord. The local authority then tries to recover the cost from the tenant, but meanwhile you will have had your money.

Additionally, some housing charities can arrange deposits, either from their own funds or from other charities. Your local Citizens Advice Bureau will have lists of charities operating in your area.

Ex-services charities, such as SSAFA (Forces Help), can sometimes provide deposits for old comrades who have fallen on hard times. They may treat the deposit as a gift to the individual, not a loan, which means that if you have to use the deposit, SSAFA will not ask you for their money back.

Remember that a deposit is the tenant's money, not yours. You might have recourse to it in future, but for the moment you can't touch it. Recognised letting agents keep deposit money separate from their own money, and so should you.

It is wise, therefore, to put your tenant's deposit in an interest-bearing account which is separate from your own finances. Who gets the interest on the money is a matter to be agreed between you and your tenant.

We know a few saintly landlords who pick accounts that pay high interest and pass on to their departing tenants the interest their deposits have earned, but this is, of course, optional. Intelligent Finance, for example, currently operates a high interest account which enables you to keep money in several different 'jars' with names chosen by you. You might consider opening one of these with your tenant's first name and keeping the monthly statement in your file.

PART 3
THE NITTY GRITTY

Getting down to business

You and the tenant need to agree on the following:

o **The extent of the property included in the letting.**
This may seem blindingly obvious, but will the
letting include the garage, the cellar, the locked
shed where you store your valuable tools, etc?

o **What contents are included in the letting.** See our
advice on inventories (p 119).

o **Who the tenant(s) will be.** You should include in
the Tenancy Agreement as joint and several tenants
all the *adults* who will occupy the property. This
may, for example, include husband, wife, elderly
parent, grown-up son and son's live-in girlfriend.
Your tenants' visitors do not count. Nor do children
under 18.

o **The length of the initial fixed period.** Since you
cannot get the property back for six months unless
the tenant breaks their agreement, we suggest that
there should be an **initial fixed period** and that this
should be not less than six months.

o **The amount of rent, and the date it is due each
month.** Our Tenancy Agreement requires the tenant
to pay the rent monthly. If you want the rent to be
paid by standing order, your tenant should
complete a standing order form (they should ask
their bank to supply one).

o **The amount of deposit.** The deposit will be
refundable, unless your tenant fails to keep their
side of the agreement.

○ **Who is liable for council tax, water rates, TV licence, gas, oil, electricity and telephone.** Our Agreement stipulates that the tenant will pay all of these. If you want to make other arrangements, you need to add the following words to Clause E of the Tenancy Agreement:

'The Landlord is to pay [council tax/water rates for the property] [charges for oil/gas/electricity supplied to the property]'.

○ **Whether children or pets may live at the property.** Our Agreement, as it stands, does not allow pets unless you agree. As we said before, you can always look at the individual case and judge for yourself – one child but not seven; a cat but not a pack of hounds, perhaps!

○ **Who is responsible for repairs, redecoration, etc.** Our Tenancy Agreement obliges the tenant to keep the interior of the property clean, tidy and in good decorative order and to keep equipment and appliances in good repair. They are not expected to improve your property or its contents. You remain responsible for structural repairs – except for any made necessary by the tenant's damage to your property.

○ **What state the property must be in when it is handed back.** The tenant must hand everything back in the same condition as when the letting began. If extra work is required to restore anything to its original condition, our Tenancy Agreement provides for professional cleaning of carpets, curtains, etc, to be paid for from the tenant's deposit.

○ **The inventory.** You will find a sample inventory on p 120 and on our website, and you should 'top and tail' it to suit.

Completing the Tenancy Agreement

You have chosen your tenant and taken up references. It is now time to go through the legal formalities. Read these instructions carefully, then follow them meticulously, step by step. *Do not cut corners.*

Now print off the following from the website:

o   **Tenancy Agreement (Original)** – marked **Original** in top right hand corner.

o   **Tenancy Agreement (Duplicate)** – marked **Duplicate** in top right hand corner.

You cannot afford to be slapdash about this. To protect your legal rights you *must* follow the instructions below. Refer to the worked example (p 106) for guidance.

Making sure you get everything right – names, addresses, postcode, dates – fill in the original and duplicate Agreements with

o   **name and address of Landlord(s)** including all co-owners

o   **name(s) of Tenant(s)** – include all adults who will occupy the property

o   **property address**

o   **initial period** (we suggest not less than six months)

o   **amount of rent**

o   **date** on which rent is due each month

o   **deposit**

o   **variations (if any) of standard letting provision** (if none, state 'none')

o   **Inventory** (two copies) – then attach one copy to the original agreement and the other to the duplicate. See p 120 for a sample inventory. You can find this as a Word version on he website – use it as a basis for your own inventory.

You can now deal with the Tenancy Agreement as follows:

You:

o   sign and date the original Agreement only;

o   sign the Inventory.

The tenant(s):

o   signs and dates the duplicate Agreement only;

o   signs the Inventory.

If you are dealing with more than one tenant, all tenants must sign the duplicate Agreement and the Inventory.

Now **you**:

o   give the Tenant(s) the original Agreement, signed by you;

o   take from the Tenant(s) the duplicate Agreement(s), signed by them;

o   collect the deposit(s) and give receipt(s) (look at the sample on p 132);

o   collect the first instalment of the rent and give a receipt (you will find a sample on p 131 as well as on the website);

o   hand over the key(s).

We know a new landlord who had a dry run of this procedure with a friend, to be sure of getting it right when it came to the real thing.

In Chapter 17 we have explained the Standard Letting Provisions principally for your benefit. Consider giving your tenant(s) a copy of the explanation to keep.

Congratulations! You have a legally binding Tenancy Agreement.

Don't leave it up to your tenant to keep officials and utilities informed. They might forget. See the checklist below.

Before the tenant moves in

Here is your checklist of things to do before the tenant moves in.

o   Take electricity meter reading, ask for a bill to today's date and inform supplier of name of new occupant.

o   Take gas meter reading, ask for a bill to today's date and inform supplier of name of new occupant.

o   Take your water meter reading (if applicable). In any case, inform water supplier of name of new occupant.

o   Call the council tax department and inform them of name of the new occupant.

o   Make or update your Inventory.

Now arrange to visit the property with your tenant.

o   Show where cleaning materials, spare light bulbs, hoover, etc are.

o   Go over procedure for emergencies.

o   Show electricity turn-off point.

o   Show gas turn-off point.

o   Show water turn-off point.

o   Show how to operate and maintain fire safety equipment, for example smoke alarms.

o   Show how to operate gas or electric fires.

o   Show how to operate appliances (washer, cooker, fridge, microwave, water softener, power shower, whatever) and show where to find instruction books.

o   Show how to operate central heating and hand over instruction book.

o   Show how to operate window safety catches, etc.

o   Go over procedure for security, intruder alarms, etc and hand over any instruction books.

o   Go over arrangements for your inspection visits.

o   Hand over keys and say where a spare key may be found in an emergency (for example, with a trusted neighbour).

o   Hand over tenant's checklist (see below).

o   Hand over record book.

o   Hand over a 'welcome pack'. Suggested contents: fresh milk, sugar, tea, coffee, a loaf of bread, butter and maybe a bottle of wine, a bunch of flowers or a lettuce from your garden – whatever it takes to make them feel wanted.

Few tenants will take in all the information you throw at them during your welcome visit. It is sensible, therefore, to provide them with a list to stick inside a cupboard door or onto a corkboard for easy reference. You might include:

o Your contact details.

o Where to find the turn-off points for gas, electricity and water.

o Contact numbers for utilities and council.

o Other contact numbers where appropriate – for example, plumber, CORGI installer, etc in case you are on holiday when disaster strikes.

o A list of instruction manuals, etc provided.

o A reminder of what repairs, etc they are responsible for (we suggest you hand over a set of working appliances and then make the tenant responsible for keeping them working).

o Name and contact details of keyholder.

o A reminder of the date rent is due.

This may seem very detailed and a great nuisance, but it is likely to save a great many frantic phone calls.

During the tenancy

Collecting the rent and keeping track

A good tenant will pay the rent without being nagged. However, if you need to demand payment, you *must* do so in writing and put your name and address on your demand, otherwise it will not be valid (see our sample rent demand on p 130).

If your tenants pay their rent weekly (or if your Tenancy Agreement refers to a weekly amount) you are *required by law* to provide your tenant with a rent book. Buy a proper one from a stationers. An old exercise book won't do!

It is, of course, sensible to keep an up to date account of rent payments, however the rent is paid. Even if *you* are inclined to be relaxed about record keeping, the Inland Revenue will expect you to keep all your records for at least six years, so you had better start as you mean to go on – and that means being organised.

o   Print off several receipts for rent (use the sample on p 131 and the blank on our website). Give receipts and keep copies, even if the rent is paid direct into your bank account.

o   Buy yourself a sturdy file. Write on it the address of the property in thick black felt tip and your tenant's name. You will need to open a new file for each new tenant.

Inside the front cover write:

o   contact details for your tenant;

o   the date the tenancy started;

o   the amount of deposit paid;

o   the amount of rent.

In the file you will keep:

o the Tenancy Agreement signed by your tenant;

o the Inventory signed by your tenant;

o your tenant's references;

o copies of all correspondence;

o copies of all relevant documents, for example, gas safety certificate;

o details of any expenditure (for example, invoices – vital if you are to claim it against tax).

As time goes by, you will build up quite a dossier. You may like to use the list on p 82 to record useful details – reference numbers for the council and the various utilities, details of any repairs, etc – all with the minimum of effort.

We know an experienced landlord with several properties who issues each new tenant with an A5 hardback notebook. On the flyleaf of this 'log book' go:

o the tenant's name;

o date of arrival;

o date rent is payable each month;

o amount of rent and deposit paid;

o any notes (for example, 'water included').

On the left of each double page spread, the tenant writes down anything that needs attention, while the right-hand side does double duty as a record of rent paid and action taken to rectify any defects. That way, both landlord and tenant have an ongoing record.

Increasing the rent

o You can *agree* a rent increase with your tenant at any time.

o You cannot *impose* a rent increase during the initial fixed period or during the first year, whichever is longer. After that, unless the tenant agrees your proposed increase:

– you must use a special form, Form 4A, snappily entitled *Housing Act 1988, Section 13(2) – Landlord's Notice proposing a new rent under an Assured Shorthold Tenancy*. You can download this form from the Office of the

Deputy Prime Minister – see 'Useful contacts' for details;

– you must give the tenant one month's **notice** of the increase (the tenant may appeal to the Rent Assessment Committee). The Committee usually consists of two or three people: typically a lawyer, a property valuer and a lay person. They are independent of both central and local government and there is no appeal against their decision except on a point of law;

– you must leave 12 months between increases.

Other changes to the tenancy

o   You can *agree* changes to the tenancy at any time.

o   You cannot *impose* changes during the initial fixed period. After that, unless the tenant agrees your proposed change you must use a special form, called *Notice proposing different terms for a Statutory Periodic Tenancy*. You can obtain this from your local Rent Assessment Committee (see 'Useful contacts').

15

Parting company

It needs goodwill on both sides to make a letting work. If you are faced with an irreconcilable dispute, the most straightforward solution is for you to exercise your right to repossess the property.

Try within reason to avoid court proceedings, which can be lengthy, stressful and expensive.

Getting them out – repossession

Most tenants pay their rent in full and on time and leave on the appointed date. The next section deals with those who do not!

Unless your tenants have seriously and persistently let you down (the most obvious way being by failing to pay the rent), you cannot repossess your property until the end of the initial fixed period. Even then, you can't step straight back into the property just because the initial period has ended – you must serve a **statutory notice**, the Landlord's Notice of Intention to Apply for Possession.

Although this is a statutory notice (that is, the period of notice and the information the document contains are laid down by law), the law does not prescribe the precise wording – use our Notice on p 133 and you'll be OK.

Now here is a step-by-step guide to repossessing your property by notice, which you may choose to follow whether or not your tenants have kept their side of the bargain.

Take two copies of the Notice and fill in:

○ **name and address of tenant**

If there is more than one tenant, include the names of all adult tenants. Their address will usually be the address of the rental property, unless they have moved out.

○ **your name and address**

○ **address of the rental property**

○ **possession date**

If you are serving the notice within a fixed period of the tenancy (whether the initial fixed period or a further fixed period), the possession date must not be earlier than two months from the date the tenant receives your notice. For safety's sake, allow an extra week – a total of two months, one week.

Example: The fixed period is January 1 to June 30. So, to get them out immediately the fixed period comes to an end, you need to serve the notice no later than April 30 – but for safety's sake, do so by April 23.

If you are serving the notice after any fixed period has ended, the possession date must be the *day before the rent is next due*, plus two months, although if the rent is next due within seven days we suggest you add another month for safety's sake.

Example: The fixed period has expired. The tenancy continues. The tenant pays the rent on the first day of each month. The day before that is the last day of the previous month. Add two months. So if you serve notice on June 10, the earliest possession date will be August 31.

○ **date**

○ **your signature**

You can now serve the notice on the tenants. There are two ways of doing this:

○ in person – this may not be practicable, for example, if you are living a long distance away. It may also require bottle;

○ by first-class post, recorded delivery.

Lawyers *serve* documents that other people send, deliver or hand over. It comes to the same thing. Don't let it worry you.

In person

Give the tenant – or all of them if you have more than one – both copies of the Notice and get them to sign one copy and return it to you. They keep the other copy.

By post

Send both copies by recorded delivery, and in a covering letter ask the tenants to sign and return one copy. Provide a stamped addressed envelope for this. The clerk in the post office will give you a stamped recorded delivery slip. Keep the slip as proof of posting.

When the tenants leave

This section applies equally to all tenants, good and bad.

Before moving day

o   Arrange to inspect the property.
o   Check the contents against the Inventory.

On moving day

o   Return the deposit to the tenants, less any deductions for
   –   unpaid rent
   –   damage
   –   missing items
   –   cleaning costs.

---

1   If you do deduct something from the deposit, give the tenant a written calculation showing how you have arrived at your figures.

2   Make sure you get a forwarding address.

3   Tenants may have had duplicate keys made, which could get into the wrong hands. If in doubt, change the locks. If your

locks are so constructed, you may be able to change the *barrel* of the lock. This is cheaper and less messy than changing the whole lock (you may be able to DIY) and just as effective.

If the tenant(s) refuse to budge – or if they fail in any other way to keep their part of the bargain – you may need to apply to a court for an order compelling them to leave.

Remember, it is a criminal offence to harass your tenants, or to remove them without a court order. Even when you have the court order, you can't take matters into your own hands. If the tenants won't comply with it, you must instruct the court bailiffs to evict them for you.

You could face a massive compensation claim and unwelcome exposure in the tabloid press if you take the law into your own hands.

There is, at the time of writing, a 'quickie' procedure (whose longwinded name is the 'accelerated possession procedure under County Court Rules [CCR] Order 49') for the swift repossession of property let on an AST. No court hearing is necessary. However, there are two snags with the quickie procedure.

o   An application under the quickie procedure cannot include a claim for rent arrears. This gives you a choice. You can use the quickie procedure for speed and – if you really think the tenant is able to pay you – start separate debt recovery proceedings for the unpaid rent. Alternatively, you can seek possession and the arrears in one action, but there will be a court hearing.

o   Under the quickie procedure, the court must order the tenant to leave within 14 days of the date of order – unless the tenant pleads 'exceptional hardship', in which case the time can be extended to six weeks. Although the aim of the quickie procedure is to avoid the need for a hearing, there may still have to be one if the tenant does plead 'exceptional hardship'. This is because the Human

Rights Act 1998 entitles people to a hearing where there is a threat that they might lose their home.

If you wish to use the quickie procedure, ask your local county court for Form N5B (Claim for Possession of Property) or download one from the Court Service website (see 'Useful contacts').

Otherwise (if, for example, you want to combine your repossession with a claim for rent arrears), you need to start with a prescribed Section 8 form. Court proceedings are, however, outside the scope of this book. You may need professional legal help.

16

A word on tax

Well, a few pages, actually ...

Unless you are very streetwise indeed, it may be worth handing your tax affairs over to a professional, whose expertise could well save you their fees (on which you can, in any case, claim tax relief).

Before we start, we must make this clear: we do not know you, we do not know your individual circumstances and we can give you only the most general advice, based on tax law at the time of writing.

Tax rules are constantly changing and evolving, and you cannot rely on a book which is even a year old to reflect the latest developments. Apart from financial journalists (for a broad view, try the 'money' sections of the quality newspapers), consult the real tax gurus:

o the Inland Revenue (see 'Useful contacts') for general information. You can download their literature – two key booklets are IR87, *Letting and Your Home*, for one-property landlords, and IR150 for landlords with several rental properties. If you rent out your property while you are abroad, you need IR140, *Non-resident Landlords, Their Agents and Tenants*;

o your local Inland Revenue office for individual help;

o professional advisers, such as your accountant.

Income tax

All income from property rentals in the UK is subject to tax. The Inland Revenue tends to treat it as investment income – that is, on a par with stocks and shares. Any landlord who has worked their fingers to the bone decorating a property and preparing it for its new occupants would take issue with that, but rules is rules!

The good news is that only your *profit* from renting is taxable. You are allowed to deduct your expenses – even the cost of this book (see below).

Whether or not you as an individual will have to pay tax on your letting income will depend on how much profit you make *after expenses*, and how much taxable income you have already.

You may, especially if your rental income is more than £15,000 per year, find yourself being charged tax on rent arrears – that is, rents which have become payable but which you have not received. If you never get the rent, you can claim bad debt relief, but you are out of pocket in the meantime.

This sounds monstrous until you accept that the Inland Revenue have their own ways of doing things, which means that you include all income *earned* in the tax year *even if you have never seen a penny of it*. This is known as the 'earnings basis' of taxation.

The alternative, available to most (but not all) people whose gross rental income does not exceed £15,000, is known as the 'cash basis' – that is, what you have *actually* received in rent and paid in expenses. What you can't do, however, is switch to and fro between the two to suit yourself.

For further information, see the Inland Revenue leaflet IR150, *Taxation of Rents*.

When you fill in your tax return, you are required by law to declare:

o   the last year's rental income received or receivable (see above), calculated from April 6 to April 5 the following year, and

o   your expenses – what the property has cost you over the same period.

You will then pay tax on your net rental income – that is, the annual rent less 'allowable' expenses.

You will save a lot of time and effort in working out your net rental income if you keep good records (see p 83 above) of

o   rent received,

o   expenses paid.

Open a separate bank account for your rental income and outgoings, so that you will receive bank statements whose day to day record of transactions will back up your own figures.

Expenses

If you let *furnished* property, you will normally be allowed a standard 10% for wear and tear on furnishings and appliances in addition to one-off expenses such as plumbing or electrical repair bills. If you claim the 10% allowance, you do not have to give the Inland Revenue an itemised account of how you spent the money, and even if you spend less than 10% of your rental income (chance would indeed be a fine thing!) you can still claim this allowance.

Here are some of the other things you may be able to claim against tax, whether the property is furnished or unfurnished.

o   Agent's fees (but see 'A word of warning', below).

o   Council tax (if you are responsible for this – and in any case for any you have had to pay between tenants).

o   Insurance premiums (buildings and contents).

o   Insurance premiums (loss of rents).

o   Repairs and maintenance (in addition to the 10% allowance for wear and tear (see above), so you could claim a plumber's bill but not new curtains).

o   Utility service bills (if you are responsible for them – and in any case for any utility bills you have had to pay between tenants).

o   Gas and electricity safety checks and certificates.

o   Gardening.

- o Cleaning.
- o Ground rent and service charges generally on leasehold property.
- o Interest on loans to buy/improve your rental property (but not the credit card debts you've just run up to pay for your holiday in Corfu!).
- o Lease renewal expenses.
- o Removal expenses (for example, to transport contents to rental property).
- o Subscription to Small Landlords' Association (SLA).
- o Advertising.
- o Extra fees to mortgage lender, etc.
- o Any legal, accountancy or other professional fees you have had to pay.
- o The cost of this book.
- o Relevant telephone calls and postage.
- o Relevant stationery – which could include your printer cartridges.
- o Your mileage for visiting the property to inspect it and/or collect the rent.

A word of warning

As you know, the minimum **initial fixed period** for an **AST** is six months. In theory, you could set a longer initial period. Beware of setting an initial period of more than a year, however. This is because, if the initial period is more than a year, the legal and professional expenses – including agent's commission – that you incur in the first letting (or sub-letting) of your property will count as *capital expenditure* and will therefore not be allowable against income tax. Capital expenditure can, of course, be claimed against any profit you make if you sell the property, but you might be in for a long wait!

---

1   Your receipted invoices may be worth money to you in tax relief. Keep them safe!

2   Be fair. Be honest. Be reasonable.

Here are some expenses you *can't* normally claim:

o   personal expenses, such as your own time;

o   capital costs – for example, buying the property (though you may be able to set them off against capital gains tax if you sell the property later);

o   upgrading costs (but interest on loans to upgrade is allowable).

---

1   If you let only part of a property, such as the top floor of a three-storey house, you can deduct expenses only for the part you are letting.

2   If your annual letting income is less than £15,000, you do not have to list your expenses separately on the tax return. You just put the total figure in box 5.29 (2003 edition). Otherwise, you must compete boxes 5.24 to 5.29 separately. You should include the interest you pay on buy-to-let loans either at 5.4 or 5.9 – but never at 15.1 (these references make a lot more sense if you have a (current) tax return in front of you!).

For further information about how to fill in the land and property pages of the tax return, see the 'Guidance Notes on Land and Property' which come with the tax return, and also – for aficionados of taxation – the Inland Revenue's *Taxation of Rents, A Guide to Property Income* (IR150). Both of these are available online from the Inland Revenue website (see 'Useful contacts').

If you own property jointly (such as with your partner), you should mark the calculation JOINT and divide the rental income between the co-owners. Normally you will divide the letting income equally, but if one of the co-owners does not pay tax, or pays tax at a lower rate, then an unequal division of income may save tax. If you think this applies to you, seek expert advice such as from an accountant.

Capital gains tax

Capital gains tax is potentially payable if you sell capital assets, which may include real estate, at a profit. Whilst your own home is generally exempt from capital gains tax, any profit you make when you sell property which has been let is usually taxable. However, if the letting has been short term and the rental property is or has been your main or only home, you may still qualify for Private Residence Relief or Letting Relief. Call your local Inland Revenue office and ask for leaflet CGT1 and help sheet IR283, or download them from the Inland Revenue website as before.

As long as the property has been your main residence at some time before you sell, the final 36 months of ownership will always qualify for Private Residence Relief – regardless of how you used the property in that time. The Inland Revenue is, however, wise to people who camp in a property overnight before selling, and then claim the Private Residence Relief!

If you are liable for capital gains tax on your rental property, you may find yourself taxed at up to 40% of the profit. In calculating the taxable profit, you are entitled to make the following deductions from the selling price:

o   the original purchase price of the property;
o   the expenses of acquisition – for example, legal fees and stamp duty;
o   repayment of the capital element of any mortgage or loan on the property;
o   the cost of any capital improvements – as opposed to running costs, which you can set against income tax;
o   the cost of selling the property, such as estate agent's commission and legal fees.

The following exemptions and reliefs may then apply.

o   The Annual Exempt Amount. This changes annually. In the tax year 2004/05 the first £8,200 of your net profit is exempt from tax.
o   'Taper relief' is based on the length of time you owned the property.
o   Indexation Allowance – similar in concept to taper relief for periods of ownership up to April 1998 – may also apply.

A simple way for married couples to double their Annual Exempt Amount is to make sure that any rental properties are in joint names before exchanging contracts to sell. This is not available to unmarried couples.

Detailed advice about capital gains tax is, outside the scope of this book. You *must* seek expert advice – see an accountant.

In good company?

Individuals pay income tax. Limited companies pay corporation tax. At the time of writing, the starting rate for corporation tax on profits of up to £10,000 was zero: yes, 0%, rising to 19% on profits between £50,000 and £300,000. This, of course, compares favourably with current rates of income tax.

Moreover, since the recent increases in National Insurance for employers, employees and the self-employed, some individuals have formed limited companies, paid themselves a salary just below the threshold at which NI becomes payable, then taken the balance in the form of dividends, which are not subject to NI. Nice work if you can get it!

Whether incorporation (forming a limited company) would benefit you will depend on your individual circumstances. The received wisdom among accountants is that *new landlords* just starting a property portfolio are more likely to benefit from incorporation than *established landlords*. The main reason for this is capital gains tax.

o   Landlords who already own rental property which has appreciated in value over the years are likely to be hit by capital gains tax if they transfer ownership of their property to a company. Suppose, for example, you bought a property for £50,000 10 years ago and it is now worth £100,000. If you put this into a limited company to take advantage of the low corporation tax rates, you would be potentially liable for capital gains tax on a notional profit of £50,000 (but see opposite for a word on the Annual Exempt Amount and taper relief). You'd have to work out whether the change was worth it despite the capital gains tax.

o   On the other hand, landlords who have only recently bought rental property, or have made only modest capital gains, might find it worth their while to set up a company. If you are only just entering the property business, there are arguments for doing so as a limited company from the outset.

A bad decision could prove costly. Do your homework. Consult a chartered accountant – but also study the 'money' sections of the quality newspapers. For example, we found a useful piece about the pros and cons of incorporation for landlords on the *Daily Telegraph* Money website, www.telegraph.co.uk/money.

If it transpires that incorporation would benefit you, the actual setting up of your limited company is something you can do yourself. Pick up a copy of *Setting Up a Limited Company* in this series.

A note on stamp duty

Most people associate stamp duty with house purchase, but in fact it is in origin a tax on legal documents – including tenancy agreements. The reason for paying stamp duty in your case is that you will need to have done so in order to produce your Tenancy Agreement as evidence in court.

Picture the scene. A landlord has taken a tenant to court. It is an open-and-shut case. The landlord produces the Tenancy Agreement in court – and tenant's lawyer objects.

'This Tenancy Agreement is not admissible as evidence, because it has not been stamped.' Collapse of landlord's case.

This all goes back to the Stamp Act 1891, which stated that a document relating to property 'shall not be given in evidence, or available for any purpose whatever, unless it is duly stamped in accordance with the law in force at the time it was executed'. This includes leases and tenancy agreements.

As in everything else, there are exceptions. The rules do not apply in criminal proceedings, for example. The Stamp Act 1891 also gives the judge a duty to note 'any insufficiency of stamp' and allow this to be put right, on the spot if possible, whereupon the document can be used in evidence.

Judges don't come into court armed with stamp duty leaflets and petty cash boxes, and it is up to you to make sure that your Tenancy Agreement is stamped if it needs to be.

Changes in the March 2000 budget mean that most ASTs no longer attract stamp duty.

Here are the rules at the time of writing. The magic figure is £5,000.

An assured shorthold tenancy *does not* require stamp duty if *either*

o   the annual rent, *or*

o   the rent for the minimum fixed period (for example, six months fixed period + two months' notice)

is less than £5,000 *and* the tenancy was granted after 28 March 2000.

Moreover, the stamp duty on an assured shorthold tenancy of *furnished* property for a fixed period of less than one year is £5, even if the rent is more than £5,000. 'Furniture' in this context means beds, tables, chairs and so on, as well as cooking facilities.

Where stamp duty is payable, the rate is 1% (rounded up to the next £5), as long as the fixed period of the tenancy is less than seven years.

Example

An unfurnished property is rented for six months (1 January to 30 June 2004) definite, and after that from month to month until two months' notice is given by the landlord.

The rent is £800 per calendar month. The minimum term is six months plus two months' notice period. This means the earliest time the agreement could end is eight months from the date it is signed:

8 x £800 = £6,400

Duty is payable at the rate of 1% on the rent for the term, rounded up to the next £5. Total stamp duty payable:

£65.

If the same property is let furnished, the stamp duty is:

£5.

Who pays the stamp duty?

Remember that the tax is on the *document* – and the main burden of tax falls on the copy of the Tenancy Agreement signed by you and handed over to the tenant.

If the tenant does not have to pay stamp duty, you as landlord do not have to do so either. If the tenant is liable, you, as landlord, have to pay £5 on the copy of the Tenancy Agreement signed by the tenant and (hopefully!) in your file.

Assuming that your transaction attracts stamp duty, it must be paid within 30 days of the date of your Agreement. If you are late paying, the tax man can penalise you for late presentation of your document. The penalty clocks up like a taxi meter.

If stamp duty is payable and has not been paid, and you need to use your Tenancy Agreement in court, it is wise to pay up (including any penalty for lateness) and get the document stamped before you start proceedings.

How to pay up

Send to the Inland Revenue:

o   the copy of the Agreement signed by the tenant (keep a photocopy for your file);

o   a cheque for the amount due, made payable to Inland Revenue Only – Stamp Duties;

o   a stamped addressed envelope addressed to
     yourself.

Address:

> Room 35
> East Block
> Barrington Road
> Worthing BN12 4XJ

The Inland Revenue issue a leaflet, *Stamp Office: Stamp Duty on Agreements Securing Short Tenancies*, available from their website (see 'Useful contacts'), or call the Helpline on 0845 603 0135. The leaflet gives several examples of lettings which do and do not attract stamp duty.

The Assured Shorthold Tenancy Agreement

You can download this Agreement from our website. You will need two copies, one marked **Original** and the other marked **Duplicate**. You will sign the original and give it to the tenant to keep. The tenant will sign the duplicate and return it to you to keep (see pp 79–80).

A note on the Standard Letting Provisions

Traditionally, many tenancy agreements print the Standard Letting Provisions in very small print on the back of the Tenancy Agreement, usually in very pale ink. The Office of Fair Trading takes a dim view of this. We have not only printed them out full size, we have also added an explanation. You may like to give a copy of our explanation to your tenant(s).

The provisions of the Tenancy Agreement must comply with the Unfair Terms in Consumer Contracts Regulations 1999. There are few judicial rulings at the moment about what is and is not fair in this context – there hasn't been time for case law to develop since the Regulations came into force. We follow the Office of Fair Trading guidance. They issue a leaflet, *Unfair Tenancy Terms* (OFT381) and a booklet, *Guidance On Unfair Terms in Tenancy Agreements* (OFT356), which you can get online from the OFT website or from the OFT consumer helpline (see 'Useful contacts').

First, however, the Agreements. Study our worked example before putting your own Agreement together, using the form from the website. You will need to make two copies of the agreement – one for the landlord to sign, tenant to keep; and one for the tenant(s) to sign, landlord to keep.

Agreement for an Assured Shorthold Tenancy

DATE: 1 January 2004

THE LANDLORD: Vernon Dursley and Petunia Dursley

LANDLORD'S ADDRESS:
4 Privet Drive
Surbiton
Surrey KT24 3BO

THE TENANT: Nicholas Flamel

THE PROPERTY:
Nowizardin
11 Acacia Avenue
Surbiton
Surrey KT24 5AW

THE CONTENTS: The items at the Property specified in the Inventory attached to this agreement, and signed by the Landlord and Tenant.

START DATE: 1 January 2004

INITIAL PERIOD: six months from the start date. After the initial period, if the letting continues, it does so as a periodic letting. The period is a calendar month, and the first day of each period is the same day of the month as the start date.

RENT: £450.00 per calendar month.

PAYABLE: monthly in advance. The Tenant is to make the first payment on the signing of this Agreement, and subsequent payments on the same day of the month as the start date.

DEPOSIT: £450.00 to be paid to the Landlord on the signing of this Agreement.

A The Landlord lets and the Tenant takes the Property for the initial period on the terms of this Agreement which incorporates the Standard Letting Provisions.

B.1 The Landlord can end the letting on the last day of the initial period, or after the initial period, by service of the Landlord's Notice of Intention to Seek Possession.

B.2 The Tenant can end the letting by vacating the Property on the last day of the initial period, or after that by giving the Landlord one month's written notice.

C The Tenant acknowledges that this Agreement creates an Assured Shorthold Tenancy.

D The Landlord's address for service of notices (including notices of proceedings) is the address given for the Landlord at the start of this Agreement.

E The Landlord and the Tenant have agreed the following variations (if any) of the Standard Letting Provisions:

The Tenant is not allowed to keep thaumaturgical paraphernalia at the Property, or to allow owls to visit.

Warning: By signing below, you will be entering into a legally binding tenancy agreement. Please read the Agreement, including the Standard Provisions, carefully before you sign. If you have any doubts, ask for time to think it over, and take independent advice.

....

SIGNED by the Landlord / the Tenant

1.1 'The Landlord' means the Landlord named in the Tenancy Agreement and includes whoever owns the interest in the Property which gives the right to possession of it when the tenancy ends.

1.2 Whenever there is more than one tenant, the full extent of their obligations can be enforced against all of them jointly and against each of them individually.

1.3 The rights given to the Landlord to enter the Property extend to anyone the Landlord authorises to enter (including the Landlord's agent and/or surveyor), and includes the right to bring workmen and appliances onto the Property for a stated purpose. Such rights are to be exercised on reasonable prior notice and at reasonable times of day, except in emergency.

1.4 The singular includes the plural and vice versa. The generic plural (they/their) is used both for masculine (he/his) and feminine singular (she/her).

1.5 'The Property' includes any part or parts of the Property and, if the context requires, the Contents.

1.6 'The Deposit' includes all or part of it, as the context requires, and also the interest earned on it.

2 THE TENANT IS TO:

2.1 Pay the Rent when due, and do so by standing order if so requested by the Landlord.

2.2 Arrange immediately with the relevant supply company for all accounts for gas, electricity and telephone (if any) at the Property to be addressed to the Tenant in the Tenant's own name and pay all standing charges for these and all charges for gas and electricity supplied to the Property and for telephone calls made from the Property during the letting period.

2.3 Pay the Council Tax and water rates for the Property applicable to the letting period.

2.4 Use the Property as a private residence for occupation by the named Tenant(s), and, if the Landlord has so agreed, by the named Tenant's children under 18.

2.5.1 Keep the Property:

o   clean and tidy *and*

o   free of vermin and insect infestation.

2.5.2 Keep the interior of the Property in good decorative condition, and at least up to the standard existing on the start date.

2.6 Keep the drains, drainage system, sinks, lavatories and gutters free from obstruction. Avoid burst pipes by turning off the water supply and draining the system before going away in cold weather.

2.7 Replace broken glass in the windows if the breakage is the Tenant's fault.

2.8 Notify the Landlord promptly of any defect or disrepair – especially anything which compromises health and safety – in any of the following:

o   the structure of the property;

o   the exterior of the property;

o   installations for the supply of water, gas, oil, electricity, sanitation (including basins, sinks, bath and WCs);

o   installations and appliances for space heating and water heating;

o   other gas or electrical appliances.

To comply with this obligation, the Tenant can inform the Landlord in person or by telephone, letter, e-mail or fax. Where the Tenant informs the Landlord orally, they should confirm this in writing.

2.9 Notify the Landlord promptly (where the Property is part of a larger building, such as a flat in a block) of any defect or disrepair in the block which adversely affects the Tenant's use of the Property (see 2.8 above for methods of notification).

2.10 Permit the Landlord to enter the Property:

o   to inspect the condition of the Property and the Contents;

o   to carry out gas, electrical and other safety checks;

o   to carry out repairs for which the Landlord is responsible.

If there is any damage or disrepair for which the Tenant is responsible, or if any of the Contents are missing, the Landlord may serve on the Tenant a notice in writing specifying any repairs and/or replacements which are necessary and requiring the Tenant to carry them out. If the Tenant does not do so within 28 days after receiving the Landlord's notice, the Tenant is to permit the Landlord to enter the Property, so that the Landlord can carry out the repairs and/or replacements. The full cost to the Landlord of doing this is to be a debt due from the Tenant to the Landlord, which the Tenant will pay immediately. In the case of replacement, the cost is to be calculated on a 'new for old' basis.

2.11 Keep the Contents clean, and equipment and/or appliances at the Property in good working order.

2.12 Keep the garden (if any) of the Property clean, tidy and properly tended, the grass cut and any hedges which belong to the Property at a reasonable height and width.

2.13 Keep the garage/carport clean and tidy; keep door hinges oiled, and use the garage/carport for the storage of vehicles only.

2.14 Arrange for chimneys to be swept regularly.

2. 15 Arrange that at all times during the tenancy there is a valid TV licence in force for any television set(s) at the Property, and pay the licence fee.

2.16 Pay in full the Landlord's reasonable and proper costs, including legal costs, resulting from any breach by the Tenant of any obligation contained in this agreement, including costs of

o   repairing damage and disrepair for which the Tenant is responsible under this lease,

o   recovering money from the Tenant, including rent arrears and bank charges for re-presenting cheques.

2.17 Keep the doors and windows of the Property locked, the intruder alarm activated and the Property secure, when no one is in.

2.18 Comply (where the property is a leasehold dwelling) with the rules which regulate the use of the Property and the conduct of its occupiers.

2.19.1 Test the smoke alarms in the Property not less than every six months and notify the Landlord immediately if any are not working.

2.19.2 In the case of battery powered alarms, replace used batteries.

2.20.1 At the end of the tenancy:

o   remove all items which do not belong to the Landlord;

o   remove all rubbish;

o   return the keys;

o   hand back the Property and the Contents to the Landlord clean, tidy and in accordance with the provisions of this agreement.

2.20.2 If the Landlord asks, allow the Landlord access to the Property for the purpose of checking the inventory at the end of the tenancy.

2.21 Prevent infringement of the restrictions in clause 3 below by anyone living in or visiting the Property, or any animal at the Property .

3 THE TENANT IS NOT TO:

3.1 Interfere with or make any alteration to the structure of the Property or (if applicable) the layout of the garden.

3.2 Sell, charge, hire out or remove the Contents from the Property.

3.3 Deface or damage the Property or the Contents (including by use of nails, hooks, screws and adhesives).

3.4 Be guilty of conduct which is a nuisance to neighbours. In particular the Tenant is not to:

3.4.1 make any noise which is audible outside the Property from 11 pm to 8 am daily;

3.4.2. be guilty of harassment or abuse on grounds of race, sex, sexual orientation or disability.

3.5 Keep animals at the Property, except with the Landlord's prior written permission (which is not to be unreasonably withheld or delayed in the case of an animal which cannot harm the Property or be a nuisance to neighbours).

3.6 Do anything which gives the insurers of the Property and the Contents any reason to

o   refuse payment or

o   increase the premiums.

3.7 Leave the Property vacant for more than 28 consecutive days without warning the Landlord in writing before doing so.

3.8 Keep on the Property, including any garage, shed, outbuilding or parking space within the boundaries of the Property, any substance which is a fire hazard.

3.9 Sub-let the Property, take in lodgers or paying guests or share or part with possession of the Property, or transfer the benefit of this agreement, without the Landlord's prior written consent, which during any fixed period of the tenancy is not to be unreasonably withheld or delayed.

3.10 Cut down or remove trees, bushes, shrubs or plants in the garden without the Landlord's prior consent.

3.11 Use any garage, outbuilding or parking space within the boundaries of the Property to park any vehicle other than a roadworthy private vehicle.

3.12.1 Keep petrol or paraffin in any garage/carport at the property.

3.12.2 Carry out any repair to vehicles on the property other than routine checking.

3.13 Leave:

3.13.1 any motor or other vehicle or article where they can obstruct access to the Property or to other properties;

3.13.2 any commercial or untaxed or unroadworthy vehicle on the Property without the Landlord's written consent.

4 If any rent or other money payable by the Tenant to the Landlord under this Agreement is not paid within 14 days of the date it becomes due, interest on it is payable at 5% per annum above bank base rate, calculated on a day to day basis from the due date until it is paid, and the interest is to be compounded every three months.

5.1 The Landlord holds the Deposit as security for compliance by the Tenant with the terms of this agreement. If the Tenant fails to comply and as a result the Landlord suffers loss, the Landlord may take an amount – which is not to exceed the loss – from the Deposit.

5.2 The Landlord is to keep the Deposit in an interest-bearing bank or building society account, separate from the Landlord's own money until *either*

o   the Landlord takes it for a reason which this Agreement permits; *or*

o   the Landlord returns it to the Tenant.

5.3 If the Landlord has recourse to the Deposit during the tenancy, the Landlord may immediately demand from the Tenant whatever amount is required to restore the amount of the Deposit to the original sum.

5.4 The Deposit, plus interest (net of tax) earned on it, is to be paid to the Tenant at the termination of the Tenancy *less* the following:

5.4.1 such amount as the Landlord takes as compensation for loss in accordance with 5.1, *and*

5.4.2 the cost to the Landlord of cleaning the Property and Contents (including carpets, curtains and other soft furnishings) when the tenancy ends, so far as these costs are incurred as a result of the Tenant's failure to do so.

5.5 If the Deposit is not enough to cover these costs, the Tenant is to pay the Landlord on demand such further amount as the Landlord needs for the purpose.

6 SUBJECT TO CLAUSES 7 AND 8 BELOW, THE LANDLORD IS TO:

6.1 Comply with the obligations under Section 11 of the Landlord and Tenant Act 1985

o   to keep the structure and exterior of the Property in repair;

o   to keep in repair and in proper working order the installations in the Property for the supply of water, gas, electricity and sanitation;

o   to keep in repair and proper working order the installations in the Property for space heating and water heating.

6.2 Comply with the obligation under the Gas Safety (Installation and Use) Regulations 1998 to have all gas appliances, flues and other fittings checked annually to make sure they are safe and working satisfactorily.

6.3 Comply with the obligations under the Electrical Equipment (Safety) Regulations 1994 to ensure the safety of electrical appliances at the Property.

6.4 Comply with the obligation under the Furniture and Furnishings (Fire Safety) Regulations 1988 to ensure that all the Landlord's upholstered furniture, as well as beds, headboards, mattresses, sofa beds, futons, cushions and pillows, meet fire safety standards.

6.5 Where smoke detectors are fitted:

o   before the letting begins, check that they are in working order;

o   during the letting, repair or replace them if notified by the Tenant that they are not in working order, although battery replacement is the Tenant's responsibility.

7 Unless there is a threat to human safety, the obligations on the Landlord at clause 6.1 do not apply until the Tenant notifies the Landlord of the defect or disrepair. The Landlord's obligations do not extend beyond those imposed by statute, and are to be interpreted as such.

8 The Landlord does not have to carry out work which has become necessary because of the Tenant's breach of their obligations.

9 If the Landlord or the Landlord's mortgage lender is entitled to repossess the Property on either Ground 2 (mortgage arrears) or Ground 8 (substantial rent arrears) Schedule 2 Part 1 Housing Act 1988, the tenancy automatically comes to an end upon the making of a court order for possession on those grounds, even if the order is made during any fixed period of the tenancy.

10 If the Tenant leaves belongings at the Property after the tenancy ends, the Landlord can sell them for what they are worth after giving reasonable warning to the Tenant or, where the Tenant cannot be found, after making reasonable efforts to trace the Tenant. The Landlord is entitled to deduct reasonable storage costs and the costs of sale from the proceeds. The Landlord is to place the net proceeds of sale in a separate bank account on the Tenant's behalf.

Tenant's rights

The law gives tenants of residential property extensive legal safeguards. These include:

o   the right to written notice of the landlord's intention to seek possession;

o   the right not to be evicted without a court order.

Notes on Standard Letting Provisions

We have written these notes to clarify the Standard Letting Provisions. We suggest you give your tenant a copy.

1.1 This definition of the landlord means that if you sell your property, or if you die, your rights as landlord under the Agreement will be handed on to any new owner of the property.

1.2 Each named tenant is liable to you for the full amount of the rent, which is why it is important to list all tenants' names on your forms. This means that if there are rent arrears, no joint tenant can weasel out by claiming to have paid their share of the rent.

1.3 You have a right to enter the property, and so has anyone else on your say-so. This enables you to send in workmen if necessary.

1.4 We have opted for the generic plural ('your tenant must pay *their* rent') instead of 'he/she/it/him' etc. If it bothers you, we apologise.

THE TENANT IS TO:

2.1 If you want the rent paid by standing order, you can insist on this.

2.2 and 2.3 Our Agreement assumes that the tenant will pay the council tax, gas, water, electricity and telephone bills. If you want to make other arrangements, you need to add the following words to Clause E of the tenancy agreement:

> The Landlord is to pay [council tax/water rates for the Property] [charges for oil/gas/electricity supplied to the Property].

If your property is a flat, you may well pay a ground rent and service charge to the owner of the building. The Standard Letting Provisions assume that you will continue to pay these and that the level of rent you charge will allow you to recoup these costs. You can, in theory, make your tenant pay the ground rent and service charge, but remember that these costs are your responsibility and if your tenant defaults, the owner of the building will blame you.

2.4 This prevents the tenant using the property as anything other than a private home.

2.5 This should be straightforward. The tenant does not have to improve the interior of your property, but they must keep it in the condition in which they took it over.

2.6 'Drains' includes septic tanks. If you have a septic tank it is sensible to make sure that your tenant understands the workings and the needs of this form of drainage.

2.7 Crystal clear (geddit?).

2.8 You as landlord are responsible for the repair and safety of the structure, exterior, gas and electrical installations, etc. But what happens if something goes wrong and you don't know about it? The purpose of this clause is to oblige the tenant to inform you of any problems arising.

2.9 This clause applies to flats where, of course, a problem with one flat can affect the others in the block/building.

2.10 This clause gives you the right to inspect the property. You can ask the tenant in writing to carry out any necessary repairs or replacements for which they are responsible. If they refuse to do so, you can carry out the work yourself and charge your expenses to them. In practice, you may want to deduct these expenses from the deposit.

2.11 This, of course, applies only if there are 'Contents', appliances, etc to consider.

2.12 This clause, of course, applies only if there is a garden. Where applicable, it guards against thigh-high grass and 20-foot leylandii hedges.

2.13 This stops the tenant from using the garage as anything other than a garage.

2.14 Unswept chimneys are a major fire hazard, and insurance companies may refuse to pay out after a chimney fire if the chimney has been neglected.

2.15 The tenant buys their own TV licence.

2.16 This clause makes the tenant liable, in theory at least, for your costs if they do not keep their side of the bargain – including paying your bank charges if any cheques bounce.

2.18 This clause makes your tenant responsible for complying with the rules by which you yourself, as leaseholder, have to abide.

2.20 Straightforward – tenants remove their own rubbish and hand over the property in good order. This clause also provides for an inventory check at the end.

2.21 If any damage is done, this prevents the tenant blaming it on anyone else.

THE TENANT IS NOT TO:

3.1 No extensions, no re-siting of flower beds, no tree-felling, etc.

3.2 The tenant may not sell your sofa, donate your dresser or loan out your lawnmower.

3.3 This stops the tenant putting up shelves, hammering picture hooks into the walls or even sticking up posters. Many landlords say 'Put up your pictures, but make good before you leave'.

3.4 The tenant must not annoy or harass the neighbours. This covers everything from name-calling to holding a late-night band practice. This type of obligation is notoriously difficult to enforce, but you can't say we didn't try.

3.5 You can use your discretion here – how fond are you of animals and how easy-going are the neighbours?

3.6 This prevents your tenant from doing anything on your property which would adversely affect the insurance.

3.7 If the property is empty for more than 28 days, you may find that your buildings and contents insurance policy will lapse.

3.8 No bombs, shotguns, chemistry sets or portable Calor gas heaters in the house, garage, greenhouse, garden shed or parking areas.

3.9 This restriction means that the named tenants cannot sub-let your property or allow anyone else to live there. This clause does not stop the tenant from having visitors occasionally.

3.10 This protects your trees, bushes and shrubs and prevents the tenant from getting the Ground Force team in!

3.11 This protects you against the parking of commercial vehicles and also the parking or dumping of dead and decaying vehicles on the property.

3.12 This stops your tenant keeping petrol or paraffin on the property and also from using it as a car repair shop.

4 This allows you to charge high interest on unpaid or overdue rent.

5.1 This allows you to take the deposit if the tenant breaks the rules and this causes you loss.

5.2 You must hold the deposit in an interest-bearing account, separate from your own money.

5.3 If you need to use part of the deposit, this clause enables you to make the tenant top it up again.

5.4 At the end of the tenancy the tenant gets the deposit back, less:

5.4.1 any of it needed to put right anything the tenant has done or failed to do;

5.4.2 the cost of cleaning carpets, upholstery, etc (if any) at the end of the tenancy.

5.5 If the deposit is not enough to put things right, you can make the tenant pay the difference.

6 This clause spells out your statutory obligations for repairs, health and safety. We have put them in here because you cannot exclude them anyway. For fuller details of these obligations, refer to pp 14–21.

7 You are always responsible for disrepair which is a threat to health and safety – whether or not anyone has told you about it. This obligation is imposed by the Defective Premises Act 1972. Apart from the health and safety obligations, you are not responsible for any defects or disrepair unless and until the tenant tells you about them.

8 You do not have to carry out work which has become necessary through the tenant's fault.

9 This clause replaces what used to be called the 'forfeiture' clause – by which a landlord could simply kick the tenant out if they broke the tenancy agreement. The forfeiture clause is no longer appropriate for residential lettings, since the landlord needs a court order for possession anyway. The purpose of our new

clause is to end the contractual tenancy if the court orders that the landlord should have the property back. It also protects the landlord's mortgage lender – an important provision in buy-to-let situations.

The aim of these clauses is to prevent your tenant from using your property as a repair shop, parking where it could inconvenience others, or turning your property into a hospital or even graveyard for sick cars, bikes or lawnmowers!

Your inventory

Your inventory is a room-by-room record of the contents of the property. Our sample concerns a one-bedroom flat which has been fully furnished and comprehensively equipped.

Remember to state the decorative condition of the accommodation, from 'Newly Decorated' through 'Very Good' to 'Poor' and to add wording such as 'All items new or in very good condition unless otherwise stated'. Your Inventory should draw attention to anything that is shabby or damaged, so that nobody can blame the damage on your tenant.

1   If you are a keen photographer, or own a camcorder, you may like to photograph the property room by room. Landlords have been known to win court cases because they were able to provide evidence of the 'before' as well as the 'after'!

2   Always specify the manufacturer of major items. Tenants have been known to swap the microwave for an inferior model and take the expensive one away.

3   Always check electrical appliances before putting them on the inventory. If it doesn't work reliably, you must repair or replace it.

4   Always provide instruction manuals and include them in the inventory. If you have lost the instructions for something, it is worth contacting the manufacturer and asking for a fresh copy.

The Inventory should be signed by you and your tenant after you have checked through it together.

Any changes of contents made during the tenancy should be added to, or deleted from, both the landlord's and the tenant's inventories. The checklist below is for your guidance only. You will of course want to produce your own. When you are happy with your inventory, print out two copies, one for you and one for your tenant. One should be attached to the original Tenancy Agreement, the other to the duplicate.

Inventory

All items new or in very good condition unless otherwise stated

Kitchen

Newly decorated

(*Vinyl*) flooring

( ) light fittings

(*Slate grey*) worktops

( ) window blind

1 (*Zanussi*) washer/dryer model no ( )

Instructions for same

1 sink unit with stainless steel sink

1 (*Philips*) (*electric*) cooker model no ( )

Instructions for same

1 (*Smeg*) electric cooker hood model no ( )

Instructions for same

1 (*Whirlpool*) fridge-freezer model no ( )

Instructions for same

1 (*Matsui*) microwave cooker (with oven, grill and defrosting facilities) model no ( )

Instructions for same

1 (*Morphy Richards*) electric kettle model no ( )

Instructions for same

( ) wall cupboards

( ) low cupboards

( ) drawer units containing

(here you fill in any cutlery, crockery, cooking utensils, etc you provide)

.... ❏

.... ❏

.... ❏

.... ❏

1 table

( ) chairs

1 waste bin

1 (*Hoover upright*) vacuum cleaner model no ( ) with tools

Instructions for same

1 packet spare vacuum cleaner bags

( ) dusters

1 squeegee mop

1 bucket

1 dustpan and brush

Bathroom

Newly decorated

(*Vinyl*) flooring

1 (*pendant*) light fitting with shade

1 strip light over wash basin

1 bath with (*Mira*) power shower

Instructions for same

1 (*non-slip rubber*) bathmat

1 shower curtain and rail

1 lavatory (with *pine* seat)

1 wash basin

1 mirror

1 waste paper bin

1 toilet roll holder

1 lavatory brush

1 shelf

1 linen bin

1 wall heater

1 soap dish

1 extractor fan

Airing cupboard

Slatted shelves

Tank with thick insulated jacket

Controls for storage heaters

Immersion heater

Controls for same

Instructions for same

Living room

Newly decorated

1 fitted carpet

1 (*pendant*) light fitting with shade

1 (*metal action*) sofa bed

1 (*Flokati*) rug

( ) scatter cushions

( ) pairs of (*Sanderson Country Trail cotton*) curtains (*+ matching tie backs*)

1 dining table

( ) dining chairs (*with Sanderson Country Trail cotton seat cushions*)

( ) bookcases

1 desk

1 table lamp

1 typist's chair

1 coffee table

( ) armchairs

1 (*Philips*) TV and stand model no ( )

Instructions for same

( ) chests of drawers

1 waste paper bin

1 (*electric storage*) heater

Instructions for same

( ) pictures

Bedroom

Newly decorated

1 (*pendant*) light with shade

Fitted carpet

1 double bed with headboard and drawers under

1 fitted wardrobe with shelves

1 dressing table

1 chest of drawers

2 bedside tables

2 bedside lamps

1 (*electric storage*) heater

Instructions for same

We have thoroughly checked this inventory and agree that all is as set out above.

Signed ....

Tenant

Signed ....

Landlord

Date ....

PART 4

DOCUMENTS AND INFORMATION

Sample letters

The documents that follow are examples only, and they also appear on the website:

www.cavendishpublishing.com/pocketlawyer

You can download Word documents from the website and tailor them to your needs.

Contents

Daffodil Cottage
Grasmere
Cumbria

Date: 2 October 2003

to: The Stardust Insurance Company
Stargazers Lane
London EC1

From William Wordsworth

Dear Sirs

Policy No: WW/212/SGP/890/2 Daffodil Cottage, Grasmere, Cumbria

I have Daffodil Cottage and its contents insured with you under the above policy.

I am intending to let the property [including the contents].

Will you please confirm that my insurance will continue during the letting, and that I will be fully insured in the event of:

○ the injury or death of my tenant, their family or visitors, for which I am legally liable;

○ damage to the property and/or its contents by my tenant, their family or visitors;

○ theft of contents by my tenant, their family or visitors;

○ damage to my tenant's property caused by disrepair or defects in my property and/or its contents.

I would be grateful for your early reply and thank you in anticipation of your kind assistance.

Yours faithfully

William Wordsworth

Reference request

Daffodil Cottage
Grasmere
Cumbria

15 October 2003

Mr P B Shelley
12 Skylark Rise
Crawley
Surrey

Dear Sir

I am considering letting a house to Mr Leigh Hunt, who has given your name as a referee. I should be grateful if you would kindly tell me how long you have known Mr Hunt and in what capacity, and let me have your views on his suitability as a tenant, including his ability to pay the rent and to keep the property in good order.

I thank you in anticipation of your help in this matter and attach a stamped addressed envelope for your reply.

Yours faithfully

William Wordsworth

Demand for rent

Date: 1 November 2003

Landlord: John Keats

Landlord's address *   The Old Muse
                              Moorgate
                              London EC2.

(*DO NOT FORGET LANDLORD'S ADDRESS — it ain't legal without it! *)

Property address: Endymion House
                              Nightingale Way
                              St Agnes, Cornwall

Tenant: Samuel Taylor Coleridge

Amount: £400

Period of Letting: 1 November to 30 November 2003

Please make immediate payment of the rent for the stated period of letting. Thank you.

John Keats
Landlord

Receipt for rent

Date: 1 November 2003

Landlord: John Keats

Property address: Endymion House,
                      Nightingale Way,
                      St Agnes, Cornwall.

Tenant: Samuel Taylor Coleridge

Amount: £400

Period of Letting: 1 November to 30 November 2003

I acknowledge receipt of the rent for the stated period of letting.

John Keats
Landlord

Receipt for deposit

Date: 1 November 2003

Landlord: John Keats

Property address: Endymion House,
                     Nightingale Way,
                     St Agnes, Cornwall.

Tenant: Samuel Taylor Coleridge

Amount: £400

I acknowledge receipt of your deposit which I agree to hold on the terms of the Tenancy Agreement between us of today's date.

John Keats
Landlord

Sample notice of landlord's intention to seek possession

HOUSING ACT 1988
Sections 21 (1) (b) and 21 (4) (a)
Notice of Landlord's Intention to Seek Possession

To: Samuel Taylor Coleridge

Of: Endymion House, Nightingale Way, St Agnes, Cornwall

From: John Keats

Of: The Old Muse, Moorgate, London EC2

Property: Endymion House, Nightingale Way, St Agnes, Cornwall

Possession Date: 31 December 2003

I give you notice that I require possession of the property on the possession date.

Date: 25 October 2003

Signed:

I/We acknowledge receipt of the original notice, of which this is a copy

Signed:

Your address list

Being a landlord involves dealing with numerous individuals and organisations. You may like to staple this list to the inner cover of your file. Add and update as you go. If you are a serial landlord, do one per property. It could save a lot of trawling through directories.

Council

Property reference number ....

Tel nos: ....

Council tax ....

Environmental services ....

Housing benefit ....

Fax nos: ....

Email details: ....

Contact names: ....

Water

Reference number: ....

Tel no: ....

Fax no: ....

Contact names: ....

Electricity

Reference number: ....

Tel nos: ....

Meter reading: ....

Bills: . . . .

Fax no: . . . .

Contact names: . . . .

Gas

Reference number: . . . .

Tel nos: . . . .

Meter readings: . . . .

Bills: . . . .

Fax no: . . . .

Contact names: . . . .

Plumber

Name: . . . .

Tel no: . . . .

Electrician

Name: . . . .

Tel no: . . . .

Builder

Name: . . . .

Tel no: . . . .

Others

. . . .

. . . .

. . . .

. . . .

Useful contacts

ARLA – Association of Residential Letting Agents

Maple House
53–55 Woodside Road
Amersham HP6 6AA

Tel: 0845 345 5752
Fax: 01494 431 530
Email: info@arla.co.uk
Website: www.arla.co.uk

Information for landlords and tenants, agent search (who's your nearest ARLA agent?), buy-to-let schemes and free booklet, *Trouble Free Letting* – send a stamped addressed envelope for your copy or download from the website.

Gas safety

CORGI – the Council for Registered Gas Installers

Tel: 01256 372 300

Website: www.corgi-gas.com

Helps you to find a CORGI fitter near you, or to check the credentials of anyone claiming to be CORGI registered.

Health and Safety Executive

Tel: 0800 300 363

Free Gas Safety Action Line for tenants and landlords.

Electrical installation and safety certificates

National Inspection Council for Electrical Installations

Vintage House
37 Albert Embankment
London SE1 7UJ

Tel: 020 7564 2323
Fax: 020 7564 2370
Technical Helpline: 020 7564 2370
E-mail: enquiries@niceic.org.uk

Website: www.niceic.org.uk

This site features a 'virtual' house with warnings about dodgy electrical fittings and appliances in each room – worthwhile for its entertainment value as well as the good hard information it gives.

'The country's leading charitable organisation protecting the public from unsafe and unsound electrical work'.

The Warm Front Team

Tel: 0800 952 1555

A government funded scheme to improve heating, energy efficiency and insulation, at no charge to landlords, in rented property whose tenants are disabled and/or receiving benefits. Note: This scheme used to be called HEES and may still appear in old telephone directories: the number is the same.

Useful organisations

Small Landlords' Association (SLA)

78 Tachbrook Street
London SW1V 2NA

Tel: 0870 241 0471

Website www.landlords.org.uk

The vast majority of landlords are 'small' – over 90% let just one property – and the SLA is their 'voice' and a valuable source of free advice, assistance and useful leaflets. Membership is currently £55 a year and you can get tax relief on this.

Incorporated Association of Landlords

'The professional body for private landlords'

As above, you will get tax relief on your subs.

Advice on buy-to-let

The 'money' sections of the quality newspapers are sound on buy-to-let. You could start with those, then fire up your search engine, key in 'buy-to-let' and be prepared to be spoilt for choice.

Additionally, ARLA have a leaflet on their website; access www.arla.co.uk/btl/whatisbuyto let.htm

Try also www.findaproperty.co.uk

As well as buy-to-let, this site also directs you to letting agents, legal advice for landlords (we liked Landlord Zone and Letting Zone – see below) and even trade associations for electricians, plumbers, chimney sweeps, etc. A very useful site indeed.

Access *Your Mortgage Magazine* (Financial Website of the Year) on www.yourmortgage.co.uk

See also www.best4let.com ('the home of buy-to-let').

Other useful websites

Landlord Zone

www.landlordzone.co.uk offers plenty of free information for landlords. We particularly enjoyed their *20 Steps to Successful Residential Landlording* on www.landlordzone.co.uk/successful_landlording.

Shelter

Website: www.shelternet.co.uk

If you are considering taking a tenant receiving benefits, the Shelternet site offers a lot of useful advice from the tenant's point of view, as well as much that is of general interest to small landlords.

Fair and unfair contract terms

The Office of Fair Trading (OFT)

Consumer helpline: 08457 224 499

Website: www.oft.gov.uk

Download a leaflet, *Unfair Tenancy Terms* (OFT381) and a booklet, *Guidance on Unfair Terms in Tenancy Agreements* (OFT356), or order from the helpline.

Trading standards

Website: www.tradingstandards.net

Advice on many aspects of letting your property, including electrical safety, upholstered furniture and much more. Look in your local telephone directory under Trading Standards or access their website.

Stamp duty

The Inland Revenue

Helpline: 0845 603 0135

Website: www.inlandrevenue.gov.uk/so

Leaflet: *Stamp Office: Stamp Duty on Agreements Securing Short Tenancies.*

Office of the Deputy Prime Minister

ODPM
26 Whitehall
London SW1A 2WH

Tel: 020 7944 4400
Fax: 020 7944 6589
Website: www.odpm.gov.uk/housing

This government department offers a wealth of helpful information for landlords and tenants.

Their website offers two excellent leaflets that you can download: *Assured and Assured Shorthold Tenancies, a Guide for Landlords,* and *Letting Your Home.* See also their leaflet *Landlord Accreditation.*

Health and safety

At the time of writing, there are proposals to replace existing fitness standards (which have gradually evolved over a period of 80 years) with a new Housing Health and Safety Rating System. You can find out more

Inland Revenue

about this on the website of the Deputy Prime Minister, as above.

Orderline: 08459 000 404, 8 am to 10 pm 7 days a week
Tel: 08459 000 444 (when that office is closed)
E-mail: saorderline.ir@gtnet.gov.uk

Website: www.inlandrevenue.gov.uk

There are several leaflets available, all in clear English. Try IR87, *Letting and Your Home*; IR150, *Taxation of Rents: A Guide to Property Income*; and IP283 Helpsheet, *Private Residence Relief.* If you rent out property while you are abroad, ask for IR140, *Non-resident Landlords, Their Agents and Tenants.* You can download leaflets from their website, or order by telephone.

For personal advice on your particular situation, look under 'Inland Revenue' in your local telephone directory.

Checking creditworthiness

The register of County Court Judgments

Maintained by:
Registry Trust Limited
173/175 Cleveland Street
London W1P 5PE

Tel: 020 7380 0133

For £4.50 per name (make out the cheque to Registry Trust Limited) you can get a print-out of any judgments against that name.

The Individual Insolvency Register came into operation in March 1999 and keeps details of bankruptcy and individual voluntary arrangements (a sort of half-way house between solvency and insolvency). You can apply free of charge:

in person at any official receiver's office (listed in your local telephone directory), where you fill in a form and receive a print-out of the information.

in writing to

The Insolvency Service
5th Floor West Wing
45–46 Stephenson Street
Birmingham B2 4UP

by telephone to the Insolvency Service, tel: 020 7637 1110. They will tell you over the phone whether an *individual* is bankrupt (or is subject to bankruptcy proceedings) or has entered into an IVA.

Tenant Verifier Service

This is run by Experian, the credit reference agency
Tel: 0115 901 6004
Fax: 0115 992 2538
Website: www.tenantverifier.com

Index

The *Pocket Lawyer* series

Corporate Insolvency	Andrew McTear, Chris Williams, Frank Brumby & Rosy Border
Debt Recovery	Mark Fairweather & Rosy Border
Divorce and Separation	Rosy Border & Jane Moir
Letting Your Property	Rosy Border & Mark Fairweather
Living Wills and Enduring Powers of Attorney	Mark Fairweather & Rosy Border
Personal Insolvency	Andrew McTear, Chris Williams, Frank Brumby & Rosy Border
Setting Up a Limited Company	Mark Fairweather & Rosy Border
Taking in a Lodger	Rosy Border
The Employer's Handbook	Bob Watt & Rosy Border
Wills and Estate Planning	Mark Fairweather & Rosy Border
Your Consumer Rights	Angela Clark & Rosy Border
Your Rights at Work	Bob Watt & Rosy Border

To order any of the titles in the *Pocket Lawyer* series, contact

Cavendish Publishing Limited
The Glass House
Wharton Street
London WC1X 9PX
email: info@cavendishpublishing.com
web: www.cavendishpublishing.com
Tel: 020 7278 8000
Fax: 020 7278 8080